# Confessions
## of a
# Fund Raiser

# Confessions of a Fund Raiser

## Lessons of an Instructive Career

MAURICE G. GURIN

Printed in the United States of America

90  89  88  87  86  85      8  7  6  5  4  3  2  1

**Library of Congress Cataloging in Publication Data**

Gurin, Maurice G.
    Confessions of a fund raiser.

    Includes index.
    1. Gurin, Maurice G. 2. Fund raisers (Persons)—Biography. 3. Fund raising.
I. Title.
HG177.G86      1985      361.7  [B]          84-26914
ISBN 0-914756-14-1

---

The Taft Group is the nation's leading technologically based information and service organization serving the needs of nonprofit organizations and institutions. The information services division provides a wide array of data and publications in fund raising, marketing, management, and communications. The professional services division provides management and financial development services, executive search assistance, and advanced training to major institutions and nonprofit organizations the world over.

**TAFT** Profit Thinking for Nonprofit Organizations
5125 MacArthur Boulevard, N.W.
Washington, D.C. 20016
(202) 966-7086
(800) 424-3761

## A Pledge

I have pledged to contribute the royalties from this book to the NSFRE (National Society of Fund Raising Executives) Institute — a cause of special interest to fund raisers concerned with the future of their calling.

For the NSFRE Institute is a "501(c)(3) organization providing the foundation to support educational and research programs necessary for continued professional development of the fund raising executive."

I am grateful to J. Richard Taft, president of the Taft Group, who shares my interest in supporting the Institute and has therefore pledged to match, on a 50 percent basis, the royalties that I contribute.

## An Appeal

I hope that my pledge will encourage and attract similar commitments to the NSFRE Institute of royalties from books on fund raising by other authors whose livelihoods do not derive substantially from their published work.

*Maurice G. Gurin*

This book is dedicated to those fund raisers,
volunteers and professionals alike, who find
in philanthropy the rich rewards of personal
fulfillment.

*Editor's note: The names of organizations and companies and
the positions held by individuals are given as they existed at the
time of the events described.*

# CONTENTS

# Foreword

As a Gurin watcher for a quarter of a century, I can attest that he is a shrewd observer of the human scene. His observations are both feisty and candid.

He describes with warmth and wit his relationships with the leaders of many different causes. Always his keen eye is critical of methods whenever he feels the results come up short. That he loves his work is apparent. As one who has learned to feel and to express his feelings, his prose seems effortless.

You will come across gems like: "Create news by planning an event that *is* news." Or: "Don't give the client what he wants; he won't like it." He makes his points with vivid anecdotes from his personal experiences.

He reaffirms that professional fund-raising counsel must recognize the importance of:

- Being ready to use innovative methods of fund raising without neglecting proven techniques.
- Dealing effectively with a client whose fund-raising goal far exceeds its fund-raising capacity.
- Devising ways of challenging donors to give at their best.
- Having fund-raising courage.
- Being ready to share the blame—even taking all of it—when things go wrong.
- Not claiming to know all the answers.
- Recognizing and allowing for conflicts of interest.
- Severing relations with clients who can no longer be served effectively.
- Not being afraid to be candid in giving clients bad news, and resisting the temptation to tell clients what they prefer to hear.
- Learning from volunteer leadership.

He indicates what fund raising should be to qualify as a profession. He holds that the fund raiser is "a practitioner of an inexact art." But by tracing the steps in his own fund-raising career, he shows how the "profession" is getting its act together.

Whether you are a seasoned fund raiser, a newcomer, or someone in between—or an administrator, volunteer, or board member of a gift-supported agency—this book will help you learn more about what motivates giving, how to innovate, how to recognize priorities, and how to use proven techniques to advance an organization's fund-raising objectives. Read on—you will enjoy this book, as well as increase your understanding and knowledge of fund raising.

With Gurin it's a very creative exercise indeed. He gives further credence to the aphorism attributed to Benjamin Franklin: "Confound the elders, they have stolen all of our new ideas!"

—**John J. Schwartz,** president, American Association of Fund-Raising Counsel, Inc.

# Preface

These confessions may suffer by comparison with Thomas De Quincey's or even David Ogilvy's. I have never taken a pain reliever stronger than novocaine or a sleep inducer more potent than sodium pentothal. And without seeming to brag, I have never been in advertising (though I have ventured into perilously close pursuits).

But within their province, these confessions chart their own course. . . It is high time that the growing mythology of the all-knowing fund raiser be dispelled by a practitioner of the art. Certainly the fund raiser depicted in this memoir is somewhat less than infallible.

If my memory has been too convenient to dredge up a wholly honest accounting of failures, it has augmented them with successes that were due at least in part to fortuitous mistakes and providential misjudgments.

I confess at the outset that I never intended to be a fund raiser until I drifted into the business by chance when I was almost 50 years old. Technically, I was untrained for fund raising. Temperamentally, I was unsuited for it. In terms of a career, I previously was not sufficiently interested in it to learn about it.

This confession may seem strange coming from one who has counseled multi-million dollar capital campaigns for such prestigious gift-supported organizations as The Museum of Modern Art and the New York Philharmonic and who, through such campaigns, has been privileged to be associated with some of the country's foremost philanthropists.

It may seem even stranger by my admission that I became a fund-raising consultant without ever actually having conducted a campaign.

Fund raisers of my age and older—particularly those who practiced in the 1930s and 1940s—had no preparation other than on-the-job training, for then there were no courses in fund raising at educational institutions. They drifted into fund raising from a variety of other occupations.

The late Carl A. Kersting, whose firm (Kersting, Brown) in decades past served such clients as Harvard, Yale, and Princeton, was not atypical; previously, he had been a real estate developer and had owned an automobile dealership. Many of his colleagues had come from the YMCA and the ministry.

My own previous experience was helpful to me when I entered fund raising. From five years as a newspaperman on the late *Philadelphia Record*, I learned at least two things: how to find out what I need to know quickly, and how to write a story in more ways than one.

And from 14 years in public relations, I learned something that many newspapermen don't know: how to create news by planning an event that is news. But I also never lost the newspaperman's view of public relations as somewhat degrading.

Neither newspaper work nor public relations, however, led me to fund raising (chance and psychoanalysis did that, as I will soon relate). Indeed, fund raising requires a distinctive point of view that is not present in either of the other disciplines.

Within 12 years, I rose from free-lance fund-raising writer to president of a fund-raising counseling firm that operated out of offices in New York, Philadelphia, and Los Angeles, and served simultaneously more than 50 institutions in the fields of education, culture, health, and welfare. And in 1972, I formed my present firm, The Gurin Group, Inc.

Looking back, I confess I am amazed at how far and how quickly I advanced in a business completely new to me and at an age when men usually are firmly established in their life's work. I'm tempted at times to consider my first 50 years wasted, but it all may have counted in ways that were not always apparent.

My development as a fund raiser is recounted in the belief that it has special interest for those entering or laboring in the fund-raising field because it depicts an actual career in the making, because it traces the specific steps one fund raiser took to advance in the business.

The fund-raising experiences related in the chapters that follow are largely about the volunteer leaders of a goodly number of privately supported institutions serving the public interest—philanthropists whose names may be widely recognized but whose actual services to their institutions may be known only to relatively few friends and associates.

My reminiscences of them at work in philanthropy may well provide the basis for the broadest interest in this book, and the personal odyssey may serve mainly as the time frame by which these memories are arranged.

I believe the most important function of professional (paid) fund raisers is to advise and assist volunteers in meeting their fund-raising responsibilities. To be of significant assistance to volunteers, professional fund raisers cannot reliably be guided by theory nor can they relate to them en masse.

With no embarrassment and not without some pride, I confess that whatever I know in this regard I have learned from volunteer leaders, many of whom are recalled in this memoir with affection and gratitude.

**Maurice G. Gurin**
**New York City**

# 1

# Breaking into Fund Raising

In 1957, I was getting nowhere in public relations and deriving little satisfaction or compensation from it. I was depressed, and for good reason: my repeated efforts to improve my situation—or even to understand why I wasn't able to change it—had proved completely ineffectual. Eventually, it occurred to me that I couldn't be my own doctor, that I needed outside help.

So I went to a psychoanalyst. I described my problem in brief and asked him how long he thought I would need therapy.

"How can I know?" he said. "We'll have to see."

"But you must have some notion," I persisted. "A year?"

"A year. Two years. . ."

"Two years! Why in two years I'll be 48 years old," I said in a voice that barely disguised the alarm I felt.

"You'll be 48 in two years anyway," he said, settling that concern.

I did, in fact, see him for about two years on a once-a-week schedule. It cost me $3,600—a considerable expenditure for me then. But from the discipline of having to focus on myself regularly and hearing my well-worn excuses dismissed, I came up with an insight that was well worth the investment. . .

I had been playing it, as they say in poker, too close to the vest. I had been tight, insecure, unwilling to accept some element of calculated risk. I felt I had to have every aspect of a situation in control before I could make a move. Most of this, of course, had not been clear to me because it was on a subconscious level.

Through this insight, I came to see that practically nothing worthwhile is ever achieved without some element of risk. And what I learned began to pay off for me before the second year of my analysis was over and in my 14th—and last—year as a marginal practitioner of public relations.

Quite by chance, I was asked whether I could write a corporate appeal brochure for United Cerebral Palsy Associations, the national voluntary health organization headed by Leonard H. Goldenson, board chairman of American Broadcasting Companies.

I said I could. The question was fortuitously phrased in my behalf. If I had been asked if I had any experience in writing such a brochure, I would have had to say I had not.

Unknown to me, national voluntary health agencies then generally observed a kind of social work prohibition against showing or naming a victim of a health problem. I blithely did both, and in the process paid tribute to the victim.

"Emik Avakian cannot use his hands, but he invented a typewriter that can be operated by breathing," I said on the front cover of the brochure. My text went on to explain that the invention was dramatic evidence of how successfully Emik had overcome his handicap and become self-supporting—which was impressive to American business and, indeed, to all segments of our society.

Not knowing the "rule," I broke it—and, as it turned out, successfully. I became an expert and an authority on fund-raising materials because I was ignorant of their requirements and because I accepted the risk of an assignment for which I had no preparation.

It was a heady experience; and in a second assignment from the organization, I continued to take risks. I recalled from the last chapter of James Joyce's *Ulysses* how Molly Bloom ended her long internal monologue with: "and yes I said yes I will Yes." So on the cover of a brochure for individuals capable of making large gifts, I wrote: ". . . and you said YES." In effect, I started with the conclusion: the favorable response of the prospective donor after he had read the appeal.

The closing section of the brochure noted the presumption in replying for the prospective donor and added: "But we didn't presume much, really, for as your neighbors we think we know you pretty well; we knew that you would answer YES."

2

\*　　\*　　\*

On the strength of these brochures, I got a juicy assignment from Carleton E. Cameron, vice president for support activities at Memorial Sloan-Kettering Cancer Center. He said he wanted a case statement to convince the Center's volunteer leaders, philanthropists including Alfred P. Sloan and Laurance Rockefeller, to raise $56.6 million, over and above the substantial funds they were already raising, for a special research push on the disease.

"These leaders are businessmen, so keep it factual," Cameron told me.

I returned to my office, elated with the assignment but troubled by Cameron's instructions. It seemed to me that if these leaders—businessmen though they may be—were to be persuaded to raise such substantial additional funds, they would have to be moved emotionally, as well as by cold facts.

Recognizing the danger in disregarding such explicit instructions, I nonetheless considered that a calculated risk was worth taking. I also recognized that if I, as the writer, couldn't convince myself, I had little chance of persuading the Center's leadership.

I went to work and devoted nearly a month to producing a 60-page document that could be rejected out of hand. It was the most emotionally charged appeal I had ever written; it depicted the projected research program to conquer cancer as a "race against time—for life."

Several days after I submitted the document, Cameron asked to see me. He had two questions. The first concerned my use of the word "surprise" (in describing researchers probing the secrets of the cell, I had written that they could thus "surprise the secret of life itself").

"To catch the reader's attention," I said. "As it did yours."

He then asked about the four lines of free verse I used to begin the text:

"In the beginning is birth,
and at the end is death;
but in between is time—
time which is life."

"Who wrote them?" he asked.

"I'm afraid I did," I said.

"Well, that's all I wanted to ask." He put the document on his desk and placed his hands on it. "This is exactly what I want."

I went back to the office with a new slogan that had formed in my mind: "Don't give the client what he wants; he won't like it."

It was an important lesson to learn: even a very discerning client cannot always foretell what he wants written until he reads it. Cameron, an excellent writer, certainly would have produced the same type of document if he had taken on the assignment himself. Since he called on me, it was my job to assess the assignment critically.

My charge for the assignment, which led to several others for the Center, was $3,500—only $100 short of what the two years of psychoanalytic sessions cost me.

Princeton University was preparing to embark on a $53 million capital campaign in 1958 and needed a brochure for its advance and major gifts prospects. This plum of an assignment was referred to me by Lewis H. Bowen, a vice president of the Kersting, Brown firm, which was providing the university with resident campaign direction. Bowen had heard of me from Carleton Cameron.

It was at Princeton that I first met Edgar M. Gemmell, the university's administrative vice president, and Harold J. (Sy) Seymour, the consultant who first articulated many of the basic concepts that still inform present-day fund raising.

The brochure I was assigned to write would have to make the case for the campaign—a persuasive argument for the prospects capable of making the largest commitments. As the case had not been articulated, I started work by testing several possible formulations. I could not see making any use of the name that had been selected for the campaign, "$53 million for Princeton." It violated a Seymour principle by focusing on money rather than program.

The case I finally settled on was the importance of education for the resolution of our major national concerns and the vital role that leading institutions like Princeton play in strengthening higher education. I sweated long over the opening section of the

brochure to make the case for $53 million—a very respectable goal
in the late 1950s—which began:

> It is now conceivable, technologically, to annihilate a continent or to
> rid mankind of disease. How we respond to this challenge (and to
> others of equal urgency) will determine how we live—and whether
> we live.

I have included the opening section as Appendix A to show how I
developed this lead. Seymour considered the brochure a classic,
and he subsequently recommended me to other institutions.

James F. Oates Jr., chief executive officer of the Equitable Life
Assurance Society of the United States, distinguished himself by
the vigorous leadership he brought to the chairmanship of that
campaign; for many years thereafter the Princeton campaign was
cited as a model for other institutions. I always felt privileged to
have had some part in it.

Lew Bowen referred several other writing assignments to me—
campaign materials for Roosevelt Hospital and Union Theological
Seminary—and I came to know him personally. Like me, he had
previously been in newspaper work and in public relations. Like
mine, his father had been a doctor in Philadelphia and had practiced on Pine Street. They must have known each other, though
neither of them was living in 1958.

One day, Bowen asked me if I had ever thought of teaming up
with a partner. I had not; but the idea caught on, and on February
2, 1959 (Ground-Hog Day, as Bowen noted), we formed Bowen &
Gurin, Inc. Bowen returned from a meeting with our lawyer and
informed me that one of us should be designated chairman and the
other president. Since there was only the two of us, I asked who
would sweep the floor.

It was our initial intention to specialize in producing fund-
raising materials. Bowen assumed that we would get more than
enough writing assignments to keep us busy from the fund-raising

counseling firms and particularly from Kersting, Brown, since he left on good terms. I doubted his assumption.

Bowen and I were certainly an odd pair. We differed in almost every respect, which may have accounted for why we complemented each other. Only rarely did one of us drive the other up the wall.

Our differences were not as apparent to us as they were to others—our first secretary, for one. She reported for work to our first office, which was the two-room, floor-through apartment in which I lived (I worked at a desk in my bedroom and Bowen made his office in the living room). After several months, she submitted her resignation in a document that charged our conflicting instructions were making her schizophrenic. I include her document as Appendix B because it shows with merciless clarity how much better she knew us than we knew ourselves.

I preferred to work on assignments independently; Bowen liked to involve me in his. He was particularly aware of the loneliness of writing; he felt more satisfied than I when an assignment had been a shared endeavor.

We differed completely in how we dealt with a client on a writing assignment. Bowen would submit a rough draft which permitted—almost invited—the client to revise it; I tended to slave over a draft to make it so good that a client would really have to sweat if he tried to improve it.

One of Bowen's first writing assignments—which in no way concerned fund raising—was a viewbook for Brown Brothers Harriman & Company, which then had about a dozen partners. Bowen's drafts would be circulated among all of them, and each partner would suggest revisions.

Some months later, it occurred to me that this assignment had been under way for a long time and that it must be running up a considerable bill for the client. I asked Bowen the extent of the time charges to date and learned it was approximately $20,000.

Because I was concerned by what the final cost might be for a 24-page booklet that was to be produced with wide margins and ample illustrations, I urged Bowen to advise Thomas McCance, the managing partner, of the tab to date. Bowen did—and

McCance said, "Why are you worried? We can afford it." He wanted all of the partners to be satisfied.

The client was delighted with the printed booklet and put it to effective use, but I felt uneasy about charging close to $25,000 for the sparse text, much of which had been provided by the client.

Other clients were overly concerned about the cost of our services. Bowen returned to the office one day after a discouraging experience with several officers of a social service organization which needed a fund-raising brochure. They were so worried about the cost that Bowen purposely quoted a fee of $600 that was far too low. But they even considered that too high.

I suggested that we offer the organization an overall plan of a fund-raising program, the main element of which would still be the brochure, for a fee of $1,200. Bowen submitted this new proposal to the organization's officers, and they accepted it with alacrity. I would have felt more guilty about my insidious suggestion if I hadn't known that the brochure was well worth the $1,200.


Some clients cannot be rushed into an easy working relationship, as I learned early on. My first instructor was Madame Yolanda Mero-Irion, a former concert pianist who presided professionally over the Musicians Emergency Fund, an organization that raised funds—through a benefit (the Imperial Ball) and mail appeal—to help needy musicians, comfort the institutionalized, and heal through music therapy.

Our firm was engaged to furnish fund-raising services after the organization severed its relationship with the Harold Oram firm, which had provided it with its valuable mailing lists. Appeal letters to prospective donors were signed by Fritz Kreisler, and they were so effective that we assumed the donors, particularly women donors, thought the world-famous violinist was writing to them personally.

For the first few months, my relationship with Madame Mero-Irion was satisfactory but formal. She always seemed to regard me with a quizzical look, as if she hadn't quite made up her mind about me. Then, one day, I was very late for a meeting with her—my taxi got tied up in traffic—and she was furious. When her anger subsided, I said (as much to myself as to her), "I'll probably be late for my own funeral."

She looked at me with a startled expression, as though she were seeing me for the first time. Then she laughed. The ice between us was broken.

The American Cancer Society's volunteers were feeling pressured then by the local United Ways. The Society's chapters did not belong to the United Ways and raised their funds independently; they felt pressured by the United Ways' contention that they raised funds much more economically than the Society because they raised them for multiple causes.

We were engaged by the Society to help deal with this problem. We conceived and produced for the Society's chapters a filmstrip with sound which countered "the United Way" with "the American Way"—noting that it was in the American tradition for an organization to be free to promote its cause in its own way.

Bowen and I were present when the filmstrip was first shown at a meeting of chapter representatives. At its conclusion, following prolonged applause, the presiding officer asked if there were any questions. The only one I can recall was: "Why haven't we had this before?"

Two of the six fund-raising mailing pieces I was asked to write subsequently introduced the catch phrase—"to conquer cancer and go out of business"—as the Society's only objective. The phrase was effective for prospective donors, and I could not see it representing much of a risk to the Society's longevity.

Robert F. Duncan, of the Kersting, Brown firm, was counseling the Fletcher School of Law and Diplomacy at Tufts University; he arranged for us to write the case statement for its capital objective

8

of $1,377,775 (which was within the university's campaign for $7.55 million).

The problem, as I saw it, was to take the remoteness out of foreign affairs. I therefore wrote in a foreword:

> International affairs were once the concern of only the very few Americans whose activities directly involved them in the world scene. To Americans today, foreign affairs are no longer foreign.
>
> The crisis that threatens the man in Berlin is equally threatening to the man in Boston. The success or failure of American diplomacy in the most remote regions of the earth affects us personally.

To heighten interest at the outset, the text began with a narrative, which was suggested by John W. McNulty, who occasionally free-lanced with us. It told of the threat to use gunboat diplomacy that was widely attributed to President Theodore Roosevelt in the incident involving the kidnapping of a wealthy American in Tangier by a Moroccan bandit chieftain. I include, as Appendix C, the first section of this brochure as an example of this type of beginning.

Since Bowen had been exposed to fund-raising counseling and I apparently had picked up its essentials, it wasn't long before we were providing counseling, as well as writing, services to a number of gift-supported organizations.

One of the first we served was the Deafness Research Foundation, whose founder and long-time president was Mrs. Hobart C. Ramsey. Collette Ramsey knew how to deal with businessmen. For one thing, she was married to one, the board chairman of the Worthington Corporation. For another, she played golf with them—and played better than almost all of them.

She sponsored one of the most profitable and best attended annual luncheons of any national voluntary health organization I knew of in the early 1960s. Her invitation said, in effect: I know you're busy, and I'll make sure you can return to your office by 2 P.M. Obviously, it appealed to corporate executives.

The success of the annual luncheon, and of the Foundation in general, was due in great measure to Collette Ramsey. In addition to being bright and attractive, she had the zeal and conviction of one who had suffered from deafness and had known the human isolation that the deaf experience.

As I was to learn from serving more than 20 other health organizations, every one of them was started by individuals who personally suffered from the health problem (like Mrs. Ramsey) or were related to its victims. The devotion and support such founders provide cannot be bought, and, in the early years of an organization, they are crucial to its successful development.

Another early client for which we provided fund-raising counseling was the Newark College of Engineering Research Foundation. The Foundation developed as a result of a trip to Russia in the late 1950s by Thomas M. Cole, president of the Federal Pacific Electric Company of Newark.

Mr. Cole returned to this country convinced that Americans were greatly underestimating Russian technology and that this country needed more and better engineers. To fund a study of how American engineering education could be strengthened, he made a grant of $50,000 to the Newark College of Engineering. The study recommendations became the objectives of a new Research Foundation, to which Mr. Cole made an additional grant of $300,000.

It was my assignment to advise and assist the Foundation's Development Committee in raising its first year's goal of about $400,000. The committee membership comprised the top executives of such companies as American Cyanamid Company, Worthington Corporation, Public Service Electric & Gas Company, and Monroe Calculating Machines Company.

With this level of corporate clout, I saw no need for more than a series of small luncheons, each of which would be given by a committee member for several of his acquaintances among the other corporate executives in the Newark area. Since each committee member knew—and believed—the case for support, he

10

needed only a written request (formalizing his oral appeal) for a contribution which a guest could take with him after the luncheon.

In writing that request (which in essence was a case statement), I learned something important about preparing fund-raising documents for businessmen. The committee members thought my first draft of 12 pages was fine; however, they thought it might be shortened some. My second draft, which I reduced to four pages, was considered a great improvement; but they wondered whether some condensation wasn't still possible. My third draft, compressed into one page, delighted them.

They didn't want to read any more than they had to, and they assumed that their equally busy guests felt the same way. They must have known what they were doing; they had no trouble in achieving their goal.

As a result of my experience in Newark, I became increasingly aware of how many organizations fail to simplify and shorten their case statements, and how this failure worked a hardship on their volunteer solicitors who have the job of communicating the case in readily understandable form.

For clients who needed a brief statement of their case, I would cite this situation: A solicitor for an organization is talking to a prospective donor who is standing on the rear platform of a departing train. As the train starts to move, the prospect asks: " Why is it important for me to give to your organization?" The solicitor has time to answer only while the prospect is within earshot.

An early memory from those years is of a visit to our office by the president of the American Civil Liberties Union, which takes on so many unpopular causes. Understandably, he was interested in developing a brief, as well as an effective, statement of the ACLU's case.

It seemed to me then that the ACLU could (with due credit to Voltaire) capture the essence of its case for a prospect's support with a single sentence: "You have a stake in supporting the ACLU even if you disagree with every position it takes."

11

\*　　\*　　\*

Jules C. Stein, founder and board chairman of Music Corporation of America, which was then the leading talent agency in the country, asked us in 1960 to prepare a fund-raising brochure for Research to Prevent Blindness (RPB), a nonprofit organization he recently had founded. The development of the organization, I could see, was to be a labor of love by one who had studied to be an ophthalmologist but had not gone into practice.

I convinced him to put off the promotional brochure he had in mind and allow me to prepare a brief typewritten document to set forth the purposes of RPB and the ways it would advance those purposes. One of the ways: RPB would cover the professional costs of raising the funds necessary to expand the facilities of leading ophthalmological institutions which could undertake more research if they had additional space.

This innovative program significantly advanced RPB's purposes; it also provided us with four assignments. We counseled fund-raising campaigns for eye institutes at Johns Hopkins University and the University of Louisville, and conducted feasibility studies for eye institutes at Duke University and Columbia-Presbyterian Medical Center.

Mr. Stein's 65th birthday was approaching, and we hatched the idea of sending a note to his friends and associates saying, in effect: If you insist on sending me a birthday present, make it a contribution to Research to Prevent Blindness and whatever you give, I'll match—up to $1 million.

A perfectionist, he telephoned me twice from his West Coast offices about the wording of my draft of a two-paragraph note. The note was mailed, his birthday arrived, and he was delighted to add his matching million to the $1.5 million in contributions he received for RPB.

By the time of his death in April of 1981, he and his wife had given $8.7 million to RPB, apart from the funds he contributed directly to eye institutes—and particularly The Jules Stein Eye Institute at the University of California at Los Angeles. He was one of the first volunteer leaders I worked with who qualified highly in fund-raising terms: he gave generously himself and so was in a favorable position to persuade others to give substantially.

The United States Committee for Refugees had long thought that unions should lend it their financial support because so many of their members were foreign born. But in the early 1960s, the organization's efforts to attract union support were only marginally successful.

Studying the board membership, I spotted the problem: labor was not represented on the board. I urged the organization's board to correct this omission—but not by enlisting any labor representative. I stressed the importance of getting the right one for the agency—one who could be very influential.

"Who is the right one?" I was asked.

"I wouldn't know," I said. "Ask George Meany. He would know."

Meany was asked and he suggested an associate, who was elected to the board; thereafter a contribution of $10,000 arrived annually.

This was for me the first—and therefore the most striking—example of the importance of ensuring that an organization's board is truly representative of the various sources to which it wishes to apply for financial support—a concept that Sy Seymour had been propounding for years.

The Whitney Museum of American Art in the early 1960s was located on West 54th Street in an inadequate building behind The Museum of Modern Art. It was a kind of appendage to the Modern in the sense that the Modern's admission charge included admission to the Whitney as well.

The Whitney board was considering a capital campaign, and our firm was selected to conduct a feasibility study. The study led to a campaign for $8 million—an ambitious goal for the Whitney then.

And with a contract to provide resident campaign direction (with Benjamin F. Thompson serving as our resident director), Bowen & Gurin, Inc. took the first step toward becoming a major firm.

For that reason, a few memories of it stand out vividly in my mind even after the passage of nearly two decades.

When the campaign was just getting under way, the board was successful in adding to its membership Benno C. Schmidt, managing partner of J. H. Whitney & Company, who was recruited to assist with the fund raising. After the second board meeting he attended, he remarked to me that raising capital funds for the Whitney didn't seem to be easy and that he'd have to give some thought to it.

He did indeed, as he reported at the very next meeting. He had put what he called a "sporting proposition" to John Hay Whitney, the sportsman, investor, and publisher who was a relative of the Whitney Museum's Whitneys but a trustee of The Museum of Modern Art.

The proposition: Would Mr. Whitney join Mr. Schmidt in underwriting any possible loss the Whitney Museum night sustain if it borrowed $1 million and bought Global Marine stock with it? Jock Whitney, Mr. Schmidt reported, "bought" the sporting proposition.

The board immediately moved to borrow the $1 million from the Morgan Guaranty Trust Company of New York and purchase the stock, which was then selling at around $12 a share. When the bank loan came due a year later, the stock had risen to more than $24 a share, and the $1 million the museum realized from the transaction provided an eighth of the entire campaign goal.

I consider this transaction initiated by Mr. Schmidt interesting on two counts: it was a new and creative approach to raising funds, and it showed that philanthropists like to be challenged in novel ways.

Another memory concerns the architectural design—an inverted pyramid—of the new Whitney, now standing on Madison Avenue at 75th Street. I remember when the first rendering by the architect, Marcel Breuer, was delivered to John Hay Whitney, and the sinking feeling I had when I was told of Mr. Whitney's reaction:

"I don't understand it." Despite some similar reactions, however, the museum's board remained committed to the architect's conception.

The formal opening of the new Whitney attracted such a crowd that it was almost impossible for the invited guests to move through the building. I had invited Carlos D. Moseley, the managing director of the New York Philharmonic, as my guest. But as soon as we entered the building, we were separated and I never saw him again that night. I recall spending over half an hour in a packed stairway between two floors because the flow of guests had practically come to a standstill.

Breuer's design was of particular interest functionally. It made the most of the relatively small corner lot. It didn't overpower the adjacent small buildings. Its few windows were purely for design and psychological purposes: Breuer noted that windows were no longer needed in a museum since it had the use of controlled light, but that windows made people feel comfortable.

Another memory of fund-raising significance is of the personal giving of a museum trustee. At the start of the campaign, the trustee pledged $10,000 (he mentioned to me that he was not one of the wealthiest members of the board). Some months later, after he had become more deeply involved in the solicitation of campaign pledges from others, he increased his own pledge to $50,000 (he remarked to me that he didn't see why he shouldn't become a patron at that giving level). And before the campaign came to a close, he raised his pledge to the $100,000 benefactor's level.

This memory underscores the importance of personal involvement of donors in a campaign: the more a donor assumes campaign responsibility and solicits others for pledges, the more he convinces himself that he should—and can—pledge more. The trustee was his own best solicitor.

Dr. Frederick D. Patterson, a founder and president of the United Negro College Fund, was referred to our firm in the 1960s by Ed Gemmell, who had previously served as a consultant to the

UNCF. Dr. Patterson was an impressive educator, keen of mind and genial in spirit, with an engaging sense of humor (I heard him once welcome Gemmell upon his return from a safari with the greeting: "Here's Mr. Gemmell, just back from Africa, looking well-fed and uneaten.").

The UNCF was then raising an inadequate $3 million annually on behalf of 33 member colleges, and Dr. Patterson was eager to know whether it could raise far more. In a feasibility study I conducted for the UNCF, I visited eight major cities where the organization maintained offices; I arranged to sound out the "power structure"—those who basically, if not formally, ran their cities.

The feasibility study showed that a much larger goal than $3 million could be raised. It also indicated to me the urgent need for campaign leadership at the highest corporate level.

For its national campaign chairman, the UNCF then was only able to enlist corporate executives at the vice-president level, and they served as best they could. As I explained to Dr. Patterson and James W. Bryant, UNCF's executive vice president, all I questioned was their fund-raising clout.

They shared my concern but wondered how they could attract a higher level of corporate executive. As we talked, it occurred to me that John D. Rockefeller 3rd might agree to help because his father had been a co-founder of the UNCF. I suggested that he be asked to enlist George Champion, then board chairman of Chase Manhattan Bank.

Dr. Patterson constituted the three of us as a committee to call on Mr. Rockefeller and request his help. In his Rockefeller Center offices, the full-time philanthropist greeted us with quiet graciousness. He was tall, trim, almost aesthetic in appearance, diffident and unassuming in bearing, but a commanding presence withal.

He listened attentively to Dr. Patterson's request, and his response was characteristic: he was hesitant to ask George Champion because he was concerned that Mr. Champion might find it difficult to decline.

That, of course, was precisely what we hoped. Mr. Rockefeller, however, did ask Mr. Champion. Because of the press of his current commitments, Mr. Champion could not accept the campaign chairmanship that year, but he did the following year.

And thereafter the UNCF continued to attract the highest level of corporate leadership for its campaign—and for its board as well. Since then, as a consequence, its annual campaign goals have risen dramatically, and they have been achieved.

Noel Hudson, vice president for development at Rensselaer Polytechnic Institute, asked us to do a feasibility study for the Troy (New York) Boys Club, which needed about $400,000 for a new building. He had promised the Club's officers he would find a counseling firm that would give them a hard-nosed study, since a previous study by another firm had not satisfied them.

What I remember most vividly about Hudson was his flair, if not his judgment, in driving a big white Cadillac on the RPI campus. I wondered how that went over with the administration, faculty, and students.

Troy was then a community that was hard hit economically, and the campaign goal was ambitious for the Boys Club. Our firm engaged Alan F. Hughes, formerly development secretary at RPI, to serve as resident director to provide day-to-day campaign management.

The campaign was a struggle, but eventually the goal was achieved—and even exceeded. Ever since then, I must confess, I have tried to steer clear of "quickie" campaigns—those undertaken by small organizations with limited fund-raising capability which seek to raise within four to six months what for them are ambitious goals.

Aside from the Troy Boys Club campaign, Bowen & Gurin provided resident campaign directors for clients from our permanent staff. Usually staff members were assigned by us (with the clients' concurrence) to work with the institutions on their premises but under our supervision and direction. But we did not limit ourselves to this one type of service.

For Johns Hopkins University, which conducted two consecutive capital campaigns in the 1960s, we provided an office in our firm's suite for the campaigns' solicitation activities in the northeast; and we assigned Stephen Wertheimer, one of our vice presidents, to manage the office and its activities.

Johns Hopkins was given a $6 million challenge grant by the Ford Foundation to be matched on a dollar-to-dollar basis. The University raised its matching $6 million in record time, and, as a result, was awarded a second grant in the same amount. This time, however, the fund raising hit a plateau and ran out of campaign momentum.

I was called down to Baltimore to analyze the problem and come up with a solution. My reading of the situation was that the whole emphasis of the campaign had been on matching the Ford Foundation grants, and that the focus should be changed to stress the urgent capital needs of the University—the reason for the campaign and the strongest appeal for the support of its constituency. There was agreement on this tack, the campaign picked up momentum, and the second goal was achieved.

The campaign suffered from a University tradition that prided itself on the absence of school spirit. As it had perceived itself over the years, Johns Hopkins was not a "rah rah" type of university. As a result, there was not the usual alumni spirit on which to rely or build.

Dr. Milton Eisenhower, the University president, was an effective advocate. I understood he disliked fund raising, but when he talked of the University's program needs, the funds flowed in. He was so highly respected by his own immediate staff members that they couldn't call him by his first name even when he requested it; they finally settled for "Dr. Milton."


Bob Duncan brought our firm to the attention of Frank R. Miller, headmaster of the Hackley School in Tarrytown, New

York. A Hackley alumnus, Duncan told us that the school needed professional help to raise about $600,000 (mainly for construction of new classrooms and science facilities), that it didn't have a staff development officer, and that he doubted it could afford our services.

Miller confirmed Duncan's gloomy analysis. I thought the situation needed some kind of innovative approach, and I asked Miller if anyone on his teaching staff was available on a half-time basis to serve as director of development. He had one man—the music instructor, Warren Hunke.

"Good," I said. "He can serve as the resident campaign director. I'll supervise and work closely with him. He'll always be able to reach me by phone; and I'll visit the school twice a month, for which we'll charge for only two days' service."

Miller agreed to the arrangement, which was within the school's financial means. While Hunke's background was in music, he picked up fund raising quickly, the arrangement between us worked smoothly, and the school obtained the funds it needed for construction. (In addition, the school realized a $60,000 savings thanks to the initiative of Lew Bowen who told Miller of a modular construction firm which provided a classroom-science building at a considerably lower price than what a conventional structure would have cost.)

This experience showed us that a campaign could succeed if we provided only part-time counseling and relied for day-to-day campaign direction on a member of the client's staff who could serve effectively under our supervision. It started us re-examining the basis for resident campaign direction, and it was the beginning of a turning point in our concept of the role of a fund-raising counseling firm in providing campaign services.

Lew Bowen, a graduate of George School and Haverford College, attended Friends Meetings in Chappaqua in the early 1960s and through his friends among the Friends learned that George School was considering a capital campaign and seeking fund-raising counsel. He entered our firm into the running and we were selected.

Our feasibility study showed that a new auditorium, which the administration deemed the primary capital need, was the least attractive to the interviewees who, if they approved the objectives of the proposed campaign, could help materially in achieving them. We also learned that, in a study conducted 10 years before by the Marts & Lundy firm, a new auditorium was also considered by the administration as the primary capital need and was rated the least attractive by the interviewees. As a result, the auditorium was never built.

This problem was solved in an innovative way: the auditorium was included in a complex that comprised several other buildings which were attractive to potential donors, the funds for the complex were raised, and the school finally got a new auditorium.

Most fund raisers cannot write and many of them (for that reason?) show a certain contempt for writers of fund-raising materials. I can remember more than 20 years ago hearing a well-known fund-raising consultant remark: "Writers are a dime a dozen" (after all, writers don't think; they just put down words on paper).

I never believed that (because I've been a writer?). I've known many a situation where, until a writer conceives and commits to paper the case or rationale, a campaign really doesn't get off the ground. And the case is one of the two major requirements for successful fund raising; the other, of course, is volunteer leadership.

The members of our firm in the early years were all fund-raising writers before they were fund raisers: Bowen and I, at the outset; then Robert D. Barnes, Stephen Wertheimer, and Benjamin F. Thompson. Prejudiced as I am, I believe that whatever success we were able to achieve was due to our ability to express ourselves in writing, as well as in speech. This belief is certainly consistent with the widely held view that fund raising is the art of persuasion.

20

\*     \*     \*

Running a firm, we learned early, was really running two businesses: one was to service our clients, the other was to build and manage the firm. With little if any experience in business management, we relied on our wits to keep the firm economically viable.

It certainly didn't help that Bowen and I managed to differ on most business decisions. An example was the question Bowen periodically raised of whether we needed capital. Fortunately, from my viewpoint, he always seemed satisfied with my explanation that we were developing and expanding the firm with the income it generated, and that that was a prudent way to assure that we never overcommitted ourselves.

But I must confess that my position owed more to financial timidity than to business acumen. In our first year of operation, 1959, Bowen & Gurin grossed only $33,000—less than each of us had made the year before. In the next four years, the gross rose, consecutively, to $50,000, $91,500, $103,400, and $113,600.

It could well be that we could have grown more rapidly during those initial years. I guess about all I can say for our slow, steady growth is that it seemed to have provided us with sufficient funds to feel our way in the business and even make a fair number of mistakes.

Most of the mistakes we made were in judgment in the selection of fund raisers we hired for our staff. Some mistakes were probably inevitable, and all firms made them. It may have been easier for us to err because, since we did not get or seek campaigns which lent themselves to standard or conventional fund-raising approaches, we looked for fund raisers with imagination and creativity— attributes which are difficult to define, let alone recognize. So we hired a number of fund raisers who seemed right for us at the outset but whom we later had to jettison.

These miscalculations proved expensive. As Barnes noted in an inner-office memorandum early in 1965: "We can no longer afford the luxury of providing a haven for slick or sick or hick minions of mediocrity. If we're selling flexibility and imagination and creativity, we must have flexible, imaginative, creative people."

Lest this less-than-moderate quotation from Barnes be misunderstood, I hasten to add, perhaps needlessly, that it was calculated exaggeration—intended to move us to keener judgment. And I offer two other factors that may have affected our judgment: the usefulness of a fund raiser to a particular firm was not always easy to determine at the outset, and the unusual types we wanted sometimes turned out to be more exotic than useful.

When we first started hiring fund raisers for the firm, Bowen and I focused on what we called a temperamental characteristic. We recognized that there were two types of competent fund raisers, and they differed temperamentally: one preferred to work for an organization on a long-term basis, discover new challenges, and find new opportunities for achievement and satisfaction; the other became bored with an organization after he learned all about it, and needed to focus simultaneously on other organizations to sustain the cutting edge of his interest and enthusiasm.

We looked for the second type, who in Bowen's description "liked to juggle three balls in the air at the same time."

Of course, we also looked for other qualifications: an understanding of fund-raising concepts and practices, experience with difficult campaigns, and the ability to deal with a new situation (the facility "to think one's way out of a paper bag"). Ultimately, we looked for judgment, without which nothing can be achieved in our business.

All this sounds as though we really knew what we were doing, but that was not always the case. Sometimes we were taken in and should have known better. Other times, we found that fund raisers were very difficult to evaluate, that their competence could not be as easily measured as engineers', for example. It was the difference between practitioners of an art and practitioners of a scientific discipline.

Another factor that could have impeded our firm's growth in the early 1960s was the lack of a clear-cut decision on the directions it would take. Once we moved beyond fund-raising writing to fund raising itself, there were a number of options we could take. We spent an inordinate amount of time exploring and arguing about what to include in our arsenal of services.

By 1965, we decided to be a consortium of specialists in all phases of institutional development, including studies, analysis, planning, counseling, campaign direction, writing, and public relations. We all believed that providing resident campaign direction would dwindle in importance for us, but that we could not yet drop it from our repertoire.

We continually recognized the need for a partner to take on sales as his sole responsibility, but we never found that we could afford to free up a partner just for this purpose; the firm was too small and all of us were needed to serve clients.

Our promotional activities in the early 1960s were of two types. The first was an anniversary party held on February 2, which duly featured a Ground-Hog Day theme. Bowen was the chief architect of this event; although some clients attended and other guests were capable of referring business to us, I never considered the event as anything more than an expression of Bowen's love of a party and of getting together with friends over a few drinks.

The other promotional effort we undertook was to issue a newsletter, which we titled, "Minding Our Business" (MOB for short). This medium for "Occasional Comment from Bowen & Gurin, Inc." appeared first in late 1963. Mainly because we favored a low-key tone, none of the items about our clients identified them as such.

The lead article, "The Corporate Zoo," written by Steve Wertheimer, noted that selecting corporate symbols is a big-time business involving a whole array of scientific, quasi-scientific, and intuitive techniques. It observed that lions are used by the movies (MGM) and penguins by books (Penguin), and then questioned whether they truly characterized the corporation or product they were supposed to represent. (Can a movie have lion-like qualities? Do penguins have any special literary judgment?)

All of which, of course, led to a re-examination of Bowen & Gurin's symbol, the ground hog, after the firm noted its *Encyclopaedia Britannica* description as "stupid and sluggish." The article defended the animal as being wise and prudent, particularly for designing a home so well suited for an age of nuclear anxiety.

The next and last issue appeared three years later with no explanation for the publication lapse other than possibly our chagrin over a word in the first issue that was generally considered a typographical error. That word appeared in an item about Research to Prevent Blindness which, we had said, was aiding "science's stuggle to save sight."

One reader, we reported, who was not taken in was the little daughter of an associate. "A stuggle," she said firmly, "is a kind of bird." This was confirmed by an artist we knew. "Why," he said, "everybody knows that a stuggle is a bird that doesn't know its Rs from its proofreader."

"If this has bothered any reader," the article concluded, "he has our apology for the three-year delay in clearing up this concern. We promise to be more prompt in the future." We didn't keep the promise; MOB never appeared again.

Both of these promotional efforts were more whimsical than serious attempts to stir up business. They were less than what Madison Avenue would call "soft sell." But they reflected Bowen and me accurately, so perhaps they were what they should have been. Anything more effective could have been misleading.

We resisted the general practice of producing a printed prospectus on our firm's services. It struck us as bad taste to "toot one's own horn" in print, and difficult to strike a decent balance between accuracy and promotion. In addition, we believed that throwing out a general promotional net yields few clients, that a prospective client's attention is gained mainly when a firm's representative speaks responsively to his specific fund-raising problem.

But we finally agreed that we should have a two-page typed statement of our firm's services; it is included as Appendix D. While we tried to keep the text factual and avoid exaggerated claims, I am dissatisfied with it to this day and embarrassed when I read it.

Another promotional document we had serious reservations about was a credo for our firm. Our resistance relaxed to the extent that, on a one-time basis, we included the draft of a credo in the

1966 issue of MOB. All I can say in its defense is that it acknowledged the firm's self-interest in the principles it espoused.

Under the heading, "Testing: A Credo," the item in MOB read:

> Sooner or later, every firm is tempted to issue a credo that states the high purposes for which it operates. We tried one to see if we could avoid sounding pious:
>
> We recognize:
> — That we don't have all the answers, but we hope we will always know better than to resort to easy answers.
> — That the client's interest had better come first, or we will not even come in last.
> — That we get new clients through present and former ones; our future is therefore "on the line" in every campaign.
> — That every campaign is different in some respect and therefore requires a fresh look and an individual approach.
> — That unless we build goodwill (as well as financial resources) for the client, he will have little of it for us.
> — That our staff must possess good character, education, and motivation—or we are preparing our corporate demise.

A memory that lingers with me is about Bowen's concern with how to deal delicately with an unwanted organization that wanted us. His instinct was to propose such a high fee that the organization would seek another firm. The first time he tried it, the result was instructive; the organization accepted the fee.

Usually, we indicated why we could not in good faith agree to serve such an organization; our reason would be either our inability to meet the organization's requirements or our own internal problems (such as not being able to accommodate another client).

Bowen continually tried to reduce recurring problems to formulas—rules or methods that could guide us so that we did not have to "re-invent the wheel" every time the problems arose. I must confess that I didn't encourage him in this endeavor, as I doubted the value of such formulas in specific situations and preferred not to be bound by them.

One such recurring problem for our firm was how many times to meet with a prospective client and respond to his specific queries before he decided whether to contract for our services. There were some prospective clients who did seem to take advantage of free preliminary consultation, and a few of them appeared to be only shopping around.

Bowen proposed that we meet with a prospective client no more than three times. What actually happened, of course, was that the number of times was determined by the extent of our interest in the individual prospective client.

A problem that challenged Bowen was a client's preference to deal with a particular principal of our firm. Because of this preference, we could not substitute for each other in serving the firm's clients. It was Bowen's hope that if we both were present at the outset of a relationship, the client would come to view us as interchangeable.

In all cases I can remember, however, the client was flexible only in an unforeseen emergency. Generally, the client insisted upon dealing with the principal he preferred, and we had no choice but to respect his preference, however much Bowen or I might question the basis of his judgment.

An occasional problem was a client who, as Bowen said, "became troublesome." When that happened, he would ask me to take over the client's supervision. I assumed that "troublesome" meant more than just having troubles, since all clients had troubles; indeed, if they had none, they would have no need for us.

I never questioned his right to call on me as a trouble-shooter, for I had the same right to seek his services in similar circumstances. If I never did, it was because I could never admit that the problems I confronted were beyond me.

David Shiverick Smith, the associate dean of Columbia University's School of International Affairs, commissioned us in 1961 to write a brochure for the institution's capital campaign for a new building. I prepared the document and submitted it to Mr. Smith. When he read it and said he liked it, I assumed the assignment was completed.

What I was not aware of was that, administratively, any document the School wanted to print had to be cleared with the provost, Jacques Barzun. Mr. Barzun, I was told, did not like fund raising; he caught on the portions of the text devoted to that activity.

He apparently showed our text to Dr. Grayson Kirk, Columbia's president. Both had typewriters in their offices, and, I was told, both tried their hand at revising the document. I never saw what finally emerged in printed form, nor did I ever hear of more distinguished talent typing away at a fund-raising brochure.

My newspaper and public relations experience came in handy in planning special events for clients. I recall one event I planned which, if it had occurred two decades after the 1960s, would have been called a non-media event. It did not take place—but it was reported to the media as if it had.

The Skin and Cancer Hospital of Philadelphia, a client of ours, planned to move onto the Temple University campus. Ground-breaking for its new building had to be held in mid-summer to comply with a federal government funding requirement. The timing was a problem; no one suitable for such a ceremony was available from the hospital or the university board of trustees.

Several weeks in advance of the scheduled ground-breaking, we had photographs taken of the hospital president wielding a shovel at the excavation site; prepared a press release; and enclosed them both in what we labeled a "mobile do-it-yourself cocktail party kit," which we delivered to every local newspaper editor and radio station news editor.

A covering note to the editor with each kit said, in effect: we're sure you must find these routine ground-breaking ceremonies pretty dull, so there is no need for you to send a reporter. Instead, we are sending you the information and photographs along with some liquid refreshment, which you can better enjoy in the comfort of your own office.

The actual non-event two weeks later received excellent coverage. The media, short-staffed to cover important news developments, was grateful and satisfied to use what we sent to them. And, in addition, the kit made news; it provided the basis for a second story.

Another event I recall was built around an annual meeting of the Friends of the Whitney Museum of American Art. It was staged in NBC's largest TV studio, thanks to the coincidence that Robert W. Sarnoff headed both the Friends and NBC.

A large turn-out of Friends was attributable to the mystique that television then had; they sat in an amphitheater throughout which TV screens were conveniently spaced. Following the business part of the meeting, which was conducted from on stage, TV spectaculars on art subjects, including a critically acclaimed program on Michelangelo, were shown.

The event had the very practical effect of stimulating the interest of Friends, many of whom were important prospective donors to the museum's current capital campaign. It proved that an annual business meeting does not have to be dull and sleep-inducing.

Obviously, not every event succeeds—or succeeds in every respect—as I was to become acutely aware of some years later when I was counseling a capital campaign for Teachers College, Columbia University.

In planning a dinner for major prospects, I thought that McGeorge Bundy, president of the Ford Foundation, would be the logical person to make the principal address, since the foundation awarded the college a matching grant to encourage support of its capital campaign.

The press was invited and appeared in considerable number. When Mr. Bundy arrived, the newspaper reporters insisted on questioning him only about the foundation's public school decentralization plan for New York City, in which they were then particularly interested. Mr. Bundy wouldn't comment on that subject and the reporters left. Nothing on the event appeared in the press.

The event succeeded nonetheless. The important audience for the campaign—the prospects for substantial gifts—was in the room. These prospects heard Mr. Bundy make an effective case for their support. The reasons why the Ford Foundation awarded a major grant to Teachers College were the same reasons that could motivate individual prospects to lend their support.

This incident illustrates the point that external publicity (as opposed to publicity focused by an institution on its own constituency) is not always important for a capital campaign. Indeed, it is sometimes undesirable when advance and major gift prospects are being solicited, for it can be strategically advisable for such prospects to know that they are the only ones who are privy to the campaign well before it goes public and becomes common knowledge.

# 2

# Building a Counseling Firm

When we formed Bowen & Gurin, Inc. in 1959, Lew Bowen and I knew each other only superficially. By 1966, we learned that we disagreed on practically everything. Business decisions on which we could not agree—such as what types of clients to accept and what types to seek—were made for us eventually by developments. The kinds of clients we served were those who came to us, and they, in effect, determined the directions of our firm. Our business grew, no thanks to us as managers.

In 1966, our eighth year, we grossed $183,000—up from $33,000 in our first year. Our offices had grown from my two-room professional apartment to a seven-room suite in a modern office building. We had acquired two vice-presidents and two campaign managers; in addition to a secretary, we also had an office manager. Our client list had increased proportionately.

Bowen and I had also grown. Mainly, we had grown older, seven years older. Both of us were in our mid-50s; and with our preferences and prejudices fully formed, we were even less flexible than when we first joined forces.

At the outset, Bowen & Gurin, Inc. may have been the corporate expression of our need for a camaraderie of common concerns and shared interests, for a sole proprietor runs a lonely shop. But by 1966, we had a different need; firmly squared off against each other in matter of business judgment and decision, we needed a third and deciding vote.

The answer to that need, fortunately, was close at hand. Bob Barnes, who had joined us in 1960, had proven to be a very valuable member of the firm. A skilled writer of fund-raising material (Appendix E quotes him on brochure writing), he had progressed from writer to fund-raising consultant, in which capacity he functioned independently. In addition, he was being sought by Ed Gemmell for Princeton. And so in September 1966— to solve our partnership problem and to keep Barnes in the firm— we asked him to become a full partner.

Bowen favored keeping the firm name intact; I felt that full equality required the inclusion of Barnes' name. By adding an ampersand, the firm became Bowen & Gurin & Barnes, Inc. The public reason we gave for the two ampersands was stated in the firm's newsletter, "Minding Our Business":

"The two ampersands are probably unique; they were devised to solve the problem of adding to the firm name without losing whatever recognition had been gained for Bowen & Gurin, Inc. during the past seven years."

Our new corporate name drew this reaction from a client: "Your next partner will have to bring along his own ampersand." This prediction would prove to be inaccurate; in the next three years, while two more full partners would be added, one ampersand would be dropped.

Gemmell didn't hold it against us for keeping Barnes in the firm. He had been helpful to us before, and he continued to refer business to us. He was in an enviable position to do so: he was in on the birth of many an institution's capital campaign because, I understood, John D. Rockefeller 3rd was so often among the very first volunteer leaders to be involved; and whenever discussions advanced to a point where professional counsel was indicated, Mr. Rockefeller recommended that Gemmell be called in. A Princeton alumnus, Mr. Rockefeller knew Gemmell as a vice-president of the university and later as a consultant with an office in Princeton.

It was while Gemmell was counseling Radcliffe College in 1967 that he recommended us to Mrs. Mary I. Bunting, the Radcliffe president, as the firm to conduct a feasibility study for the campaign that the board and she were contemplating. She apparently had confidence in Gemmell's judgment, for she engaged us.

In conducting the study, I conferred frequently with Mrs. Bunting, who more than anyone else charted the college's future direction. One of the more original thinkers among the presidents of women's colleges, she had founded the Radcliffe Institute (later named in her honor) as a laboratory of applied social science, a means of learning how to help more women realize their intellectual and creative potentialities.

She had been widowed more than a decade before and had a responsibility beyond presiding over Radcliffe—rearing three sons and a daughter—though I never knew it to interfere with her presidential duties. She was serious, earnest, dedicated, totally committed to the college. I never even tried to interject a light note in our dealings. With Mrs. Bunting, I assumed, it was always business.

Our study tested the feasibility of raising $15 million for immediate needs out of a total of $30 million the college required over the coming decade. It showed that only $10 million was a realistic expectation in a three-year campaign.

The study findings were resisted by all of the board members, including those whose advice to me on their own giving intentions largely guided me in recommending $10 million as a feasible goal. Because they spoke to me in confidence, I was in the unhappy position of having persuasive information and not being able to use it; yet, because I had this knowledge, I felt I must in good conscience be guided by it.

It was a stand-off until a solution occurred to me. I proposed that the campaign leadership initiate the solicitation of advance gift prospects (mainly the board members and any others who might be ready at the outset to pledge substantially and at their best), and ask them to pledge against the total immediate needs of $15 million. If these advance gift pledges came in much higher than my study findings indicated, I said, I would be happy to be proven wrong and the campaign goal could be set at $15 million.

In making this proposal, I noted that there was no need to make any public announcement of the goal at that time, that the press was not encamped at our doorstep awaiting such an announcement, and that even a $15 million goal would not be impressive to the public at a time when institutions' capital campaign goals were being set at amounts many times larger.

Because a board is sometimes unclear about when a public announcement should be made, I added that such an announcement usually was not made at the outset of a campaign (when the sharing of such information was limited to an institution's constituency), but was made after the initial pledges totaled a sufficiently large percentage of the goal (perhaps a third) to indicate that the campaign was off to a good start and prospects for its complete success were favorable.

The board accepted the proposal and it was given a trial. Unfortunately, my study recommendation of a $10 million goal proved to be accurate. In fact, if one prospect had not eventually provided over one-half of the total goal, not even the $10 million goal would have been achieved.

The prospect considered to be most capable of making an impressive advance gift pledge was Mrs. Ailsa Mellon Bruce. She was also deemed to have the necessary interest because her late daughter Audrey, Mrs. Stephen Currier, had been a Radcliffe alumna.

Mrs. Bunting made a call on Mrs. Bruce and told her of the need for the campaign's largest objective, a new Radcliffe House (which, like a Harvard House, was really a collection of residential houses). Mrs. Bruce responded with a pledge of $1.4 million.

It was a handsome commitment, and I (among many others) congratulated Mrs. Bunting on her success in obtaining a gift that represented almost 15 percent of the total campaign goal.

I couldn't resist making another observation: her experience certainly disproved a general notion then that women fund raisers were successful only in obtaining small gifts, and that they were hesitant, if not fearful, of asking for large gifts.

I was thus savoring Mrs. Bunting's success when another thought occurred to me.

"Mrs. Bruce's pledge was certainly generous," I said, "but I wouldn't call it a sacrificial gift."

"What do you mean?" Mrs. Bunting asked.

"Well, I assume it won't make her forgo lunch," I said.

"Just what are you saying?"

"I recently read that Mrs. Bruce is supposed to be worth about $700 million. . . I guess she could give more, if she wanted to."

Mrs. Bunting spoke again to Mrs. Bruce who, anxious to have the project move forward, increased her pledge to $5.4 million to cover the entire cost of the Radcliffe House (which was subsequently named in memory of her daughter).

Mrs. Bruce's commitment, which accounted for more than half of the entire campaign goal, was dramatic confirmation of capital campaign experience that very large gifts must provide the lion's share of the goal.

The campaign's success was attributable in large measure to Mrs. Bunting's persistence and dedication, and to her belief in the importance of the campaign's objectives. But she was also a feminist; during the campaign, she pushed for the complete integration of Radcliffe into Harvard—even though some of the older alumnae who could give substantially to the campaign were believed to favor the continuation of Radcliffe as a women's college affiliated with Harvard.

In a gracious note to me in June of 1969 after the campaign goal had been achieved, she noted: " 'Each institution is unique,' you said when you made the initial survey, 'and Radcliffe is more unique than most.' That was before it threatened to do away with itself in the midst of its campaign. You're not likely to face the likes of that again for some years." How right she was.

Following our counseling of the Radcliffe campaign, and again on the recommendation of Ed Gemmell, we were engaged to conduct a feasibility study for Sarah Lawrence College, which was also contemplating a $10 million capital campaign.

Our study recommended $10 million as a "stretch" goal—more than what would ordinarily be feasible but one which could serve as a challenge to prospective donors. For a period, we assigned Steve Wertheimer, our vice president, as resident campaign director. A fund raiser of exceptional ability, Steve served admirably under trying circumstances.

I could appreciate his situation, as I was supervising the campaign and was also experiencing difficulty. My problems were mainly with Mrs. Esther Raushenbush, the college president. We got on well enough on the surface, but I found it difficult to convince her on campaign strategy.

A basic principle of campaign strategy is to involve the volunteers who can make substantial commitments. Since one of the capital objectives of the campaign was a new library, I suggested that she form a volunteer committee, which would include board members Thomas J. Watson, Jr. and Gaylord Donnelley (both of whom had daughters at the college), to study the needs of that objective. She could not see the value of the suggestion and did not act on it.

I guess I must have sat through four or five board meetings, and there too the volunteer board members had little opportunity to participate and thus to become involved and committed. While the capital campaign was usually listed on the board meeting agenda, the subject was usually dealt with by report rather than by discussion; no attempt was made to plan for board participation.

At one point during a board meeting, when I happened to be sitting next to her, I slipped a note in front of Mrs. Raushenbush on which I had written, "Ask the board whether the library of the future should resemble a collection of books or a computer." To my surprise, she read the question to the board.

Mr. Watson, whom I had never before heard utter a word at a board meeting, immediately responded that a library still had to be a collection of books because information retrieval by computer for that purpose was not yet economical. But that was as far as his involvement was encouraged. I believed that if he had been appropriately involved, he would have given the library in honor of his father.

If I found Mrs. Raushenbush difficult to convince, she must have found me difficult to believe. She would continually return to the same question, which could only have meant that she was not convinced by my answer. The memory of one such question is still with me. . .

The campaign was well into its first year when she suddenly asked me, "How do you know Sarah Lawrence can raise $10 million?" The question surprised me because our feasibility study had recommended that stretch goal, and I reminded her of that.

"But *how* do you know?" she persisted.

"Our findings are based on the views—reflecting the intentions—of the prospective donors who could pretty much assure the achievement of the goal," I said.

She looked unconvinced, so I added, "Your board accepted the goal we recommended and authorized the fund-raising campaign we're now conducting."

"But how do you *really* know we can raise $10 million?"

"You'll remember," I said, "that in our study report we noted that our firm had conducted campaigns for similar goals for somewhat similar colleges, such as Radcliffe, and that in our judgment Sarah Lawrence's fund-raising potential measured up favorably in comparison."

"But how do you *know?*"

I thought of St. Paul when he confronted that question: "Faith is the evidence of things unseen. . ."

"Beyond the assurances our study provided, you have to go on faith," I said.

And then, remembering the importance of the self-fulfilling prophesy, I added "You have to believe that the goal will be achieved. Indeed, if you don't, it will never happen."

My answer produced a thoughtful silence, and I continued, "In a fund-raising campaign, obviously, you haven't succeeded until you have attained the goal. In a sense, then, you're a failure until you succeed. You have to learn to live with failure until the last of the needed funds are in hand."

She let it rest at that, though I was not certain that she was really convinced. I had the impression that she viewed me with some disparagement as a practitioner of an inexact art—which, in my view, is an exact description of a fund raiser.

A similar concern about the goal was never expressed by the board members, some of whom (like Mr. Watson and Mr. Donnelley) were certainly not unacquainted with capital campaigns.

David M. Keiser, who accompanied Mrs. Raushenbush on some solicitation calls, apparently heard of my response to her question.

When he greeted me on Park Avenue several months later, he introduced me to his wife with the comment, "This is the fund raiser who said, 'in fund raising, you're a failure until you succeed.' "

My words sounded fatuous when they were quoted back to me, but Mr. Keiser knew what I had meant. He was one of the most effective volunteer fund raisers I've ever known; he had the courage to ask for the big gift.

Mr. Keiser was board chairman of the New York Philharmonic in the mid-1960s when our firm was engaged to provide resident direction for a $10 million endowment campaign; and one of our professional duties was to help evaluate the giving potential of prospective donors.

Our firm rated the giving potential of an important advance gift prospect at only $100,000 because we were aware of his many other philanthropic commitments. When we offered this advice to Mr. Keiser and Amyas Ames, president of the Philharmonic, who were to call on the prospect, neither of them raised any objection to it; so Thompson (our resident campaign director), Bowen, and I assumed their concurrence.

It was therefore with considerable surprise that we heard what had actually occurred when the solicitation call was made: Mr. Keiser asked the prospect to consider making a pledge of $250,000—two-and-a-half times the amount we had suggested— and the prospect responded favorably.

It was this kind of fund-raising courage—a courage based on conviction about the importance of the cause he represented—that made David Keiser such a successful volunteer fund raiser; it was this ability to ask for the big gift that we professional fund raisers term "the instinct for the jugular." The term suggests the jungle, but in the name of charity, it takes on a loftier meaning.

The campaign itself was less successful; the goal was not achieved. The reasons for the failure—the first we suffered—were instructive. Our study indicated that $8.5 million was a realistic expectation, though a "stretch" goal of $10 million was worth trying for because it reflected more accurately the Philharmonic's needs and could serve to raise donor's giving sights.

But after a 33-month campaign, the pledges totaled only $7,270,000. While this outcome was accepted by the volunteer leadership, it bothered Bowen particularly because he had supervised the campaign. He therefore spent considerable time in analyzing the failure to achieve a higher total.

Among the causes Bowen cited in his final report on the campaign: illness had prevented the campaign chairman from serving long, the appeal's restriction just to endowment reduced the number of campaign contributions (some donors would not give to endowment), and competition by the fund-raising activities of other Lincoln Center constituent organizations adversely affected gifts at the middle and lowest giving levels.

However valid the reasons for failing to achieve the goal or approximating it more closely, it was a deeply felt personal disappointment to Bowen and me. We certainly appreciated the readiness with which the campaign results were accepted by the volunteer leaders; they were satisfied that a very conscientious fund-raising effort had been made. We too knew that such an effort had been made, but it didn't help us much to overcome our disappointment.

We had failures (any firm that claims it hasn't should be viewed with suspicion), but they were not many and they were not disastrous to our clients. In the case of the Philharmonic, for example, the failure to meet the "stretch" goal (and such a goal involves a calculated risk) meant that the institution would have several million dollars less in endowment; it survived decently enough. It wasn't as if a client undertook the construction of a new building and didn't have sufficient funds to complete it—a situation we never experienced.

Our failures were kept to a bare minimum by the hard-nosed feasibility study we insisted upon making before we would provide campaign services to a prospective client. It was our impression that some firms undertook a study as a loss leader—a way of getting to provide campaign services which, since they were profitable and could extend over several years, could more than compensate for any financial loss on the study. Such a study was usually conducted in such a perfunctory way that we considered it boilerplate.

Firms like ours, which considered a feasibility study a separate assignment (apart from any campaign counseling service that might result if a campaign was indicated), therefore charged adequately for it. The fee we submitted was based upon our estimate of the time it would take us to complete the study.

I confess that I was always pleased that whenever several firms were asked to submit their fees for a study, ours was the highest. It seemed to me that, apart from other factors, there was an advantage—certainly the suggestion of a qualitative distinction—in submitting the highest bid. And since we could always justify our fee and usually put in more work than our estimate would cover, I felt no guilt about it.

I was also pleased to find that almost all first-rate institutions and organizations didn't want a bargain; they wanted the best. When one didn't, we were just as pleased when another firm was selected. Meeting once with the selection committee of a college, I was asked why our bid was twice as high as the next highest. I said I was surprised to hear that, as we were usually much higher. The members of the committee laughed approvingly.

The perfunctory study that some firms conducted seemed to us to have no value ethically or practically, since the primary purpose of a study was to determine as accurately as possible whether a capital campaign goal was feasible. When a projected campaign goal was unfeasible, neither the client nor the counseling firm has a valid reason for undertaking the campaign. Thus, the feasibility study protected the client and the firm against embarking upon a campaign that was doomed to failure.

When we conducted a study, we maintained an impersonal and critical attitude. I remember being chided once by a board chairman for my cold approach. I told him that if the study showed the goal was feasible and I was engaged to counsel the campaign, I would then become an ardent advocate—but not before.

That was why I always thought it was ridiculous of some universities to insist that a fund raiser directing a study had to be an alumnus. If there is one thing a fund raiser assessing a university's fund-raising potential should not be, it is an alumnus.

Even a favorable finding by a feasibility study cannot always ensure that a campaign will succeed. It takes more than a sound study and the conscientious advice and assistance of professional fund-raising counsel. It also requires such other ingredients for success as total board commitment to the campaign, able and active leadership, the absence of other campaigns competing for the same prospective donors, and (preferably) a climate favorable for fund raising.

But it's not always possible to undertake a study; it's not always possible to initiate a campaign at a favorable time. Sometimes fund-raising counsel is called in late—too late to take the proper precautions.

An example comes to mind. William Penn Charter, a Friends school, called us because the headmaster knew of our previous campaign for George School. The school urgently needed a new gymnasium, Headmaster John F. Gummere told us. He then led us to the window and pointed to a new building that was almost completely constructed—it was the new gymnasium.

One doesn't have to be a professional fund raiser to know that it is very difficult to make the case for a need when it has practically been satisfied. My reaction was to call the campaign an "Act of Faith" and to claim that the school went ahead and built the new gymnasium because it had faith that the parents, alumni, and friends of Penn Charter would provide the necessary funds. The strategy succeeded, but I wouldn't want to have to count on it again.

Mrs. Mary Lasker, whom we met when she was serving on the Research to Prevent Blindness board, recommended our firm to Roger L. Stevens, board chairman of the John F. Kennedy Center for the Performing Arts. The Center still needed funds for construction, and Mr. Stevens was the chief volunteer fund raiser, working out of an office in the Johnson White House. Our assignment was to assist him in raising $5 million more from individual donors.

Certainly a very vivid memory of our Kennedy Center association concerns Howard F. Ahmanson, who served as vice chairman of the board. Mr. Ahmanson presided over Home Savings of America, the nation's biggest savings and loan association, from his headquarters in Los Angeles.

Some time after we began working for the Center, Mr. Ahmanson was asked to contribute one of the three theaters in the Kennedy Center; each of these three named gift opportunities was listed at $400,000. Several months went by and, when no response was received from Mr. Ahmanson, we became concerned.

We therefore arranged for a member of our firm to drop by Mr. Ahmanson's office, on the pretext that he was in the vicinity, and learn if there was any problem with the request. On his return, our associate reported that Mr. Ahmanson was offended; in such requests, he usually was not asked for contributions of under $1 million and he didn't like it.

This instance extends the old fund-raising adage that there is no risk in asking prospective donors for large gifts; they may not make such gifts but they will not be offended. For some prospects, there is a risk in asking for gifts they do not consider large enough.

An equally vivid memory is of our firm's loss of the Kennedy Center as a client. It was one of two prestigious clients we lost; the other was the New York Botanical Garden. With both clients, the reasons we failed were identical: our investigation of applicants for positions with our firm proved to be insufficiently thorough, and we did not provide them with adequate training and supervision.

These confessions would be less than complete if I did not admit to such failures. Our firm deserved to lose these clients. And the lessons we learned were instructive and not easily forgotten.

\*     \*     \*

While every institution we served was unique in the sense that it was different from all others in some respect, the Friends Select School in Philadelphia presented a development problem that was so different it seemed to be insolvable.

A privately supported secondary school, Friends Select was housed in hopelessly outdated facilities on land, deeded to it by William Penn, in an area which had become a business district. The surrounding neighborhoods had also changed and its student enrollment had become predominantly black.

With inadequate operating funds and meager sources of additional support, the school could have solved its problems by moving to the affluent suburbs; being a Quaker institution, it preferred to stay and fight to survive.

An acceptable solution emerged with the recognition that the valuable land the school owned had not been developed to the full extent permitted by local zoning, that the income-producing potential of its frozen assets had not been realized.

Acting on this recognition, the school interested the Pennsalt Chemicals Corporation in taking a 99-year lease on its valuable property and constructing a 20-story building through an arrangement which made it possible for Friends Select to erect a new school building and eventually to receive annual income for its maintenance.

If this approach was not conventional fund raising, it was effective financial development in a situation which did not lend itself to other solutions. But this was not to be the last time we would be involved in this approach. And the next time, because it would incorporate additional income-producing features, it would represent a new and unique development program.


I've found it stimulating to compete with other firms for clients, but I have always been embarrassed by one form that this competition sometimes takes: the "beauty parade," as it is known in the trade.

To stage this contest, a prospective client arranges for a number of counseling firms (occasionally as many as six or more) to "parade" past—appear for interviews before—a volunteer selection committee. Sometimes the interviews are scheduled at half-hour intervals.

Thus, representatives of participating firms cannot avoid the embarrassment of passing each other as they enter and leave the meetings. I've always found this experience to be degrading, and I've never known a consultant who didn't share that feeling.

But what is more important is the questionable value of this procedure to the prospective client. For with such scheduling, all parties to the proceedings are rushed: the firms—in learning about the prospective client, making their presentations, and fielding the committee's questions; and the committee—in gaining all the information it could use, as well as assimilating it, in selecting intelligently the firm best suited to meet the prospective client's particular needs.

Fortunately, I was not exposed frequently to this hurried and unsatisfactory procedure. Usually, I was asked to meet with a prospective client when other firms were not scheduled and when there was adequate time for a useful discussion and a full exchange of views.


Most of our clients were referred to us by former clients, which is the best—and certainly the most gratifying—way to get business.

On the basis of the counseling service we provided George School, we were called in by other Quaker schools, including William Penn Charter, Friends Select, Germantown Friends, Westtown, and Friends Central.

Our experience with the Whitney Museum of American Art enabled us to attract other museums, including The Museum of Modern Art (New York), Philadelphia Museum of Art, Museum of Fine Arts (Boston), Dallas Museum of Fine Arts, Phoenix Art Museum, Detroit Institute of Art, and Seattle Art Museum.

With health organizations, our experience was the same. By the late 1960s, we had served more than 20 health organizations either on a retainer or project basis. Among them were the American Diabetes Association, American Cancer Society, United Cerebral Palsey Associations, Arthritis Foundation, Deafness Research Foundation, Research to Prevent Blindness, and Parkinson's Disease Foundation.

I had long wondered why it was that, at a certain point in the development of a national voluntary health organization, its fundraising pattern changed radically and it moved from slow annual increases to a sharply accelerated rate of growth. To find an answer, I undertook my own study.

Concentrating on the 10 organizations raising the most funds, I studied the fund-raising history of each to learn when this sudden point of sharp increase occurred. While the time varied (the average was about 15 years), I noted that the radical change came when the organization was raising about $4.5 million annually.

I could discern nothing magical about that amount until I figured out that $4.5 million enabled such an organization to provide sufficient field staff to help its chapters raise funds more effectively. While the amount would increase in future years, its significance would not change.

It's strange, now that I think of it, that I've not written of this finding before, though I certainly have used it in working for beginning and developing health organizations.

With Lew Bowen's concurrence, I terminated our fund-raising counseling service for two colleges in the late 1960s—Manhattan College and Teachers College of Columbia University, both of which had embarked on capital campaigns.

In each instance, the reasons were basically the same: the inability to move the board to complete commitment to the campaign, and the failure to persuade advance gift prospects to make the pace-setting leadership pledges that are essential if the campaign is to get off to a promising start.

When I felt our services should be terminated at Manhattan College, I told the president that I would advise him to that effect in a letter which he could use with the board in focusing its attention more forcefully on the campaign and in stimulating leadership pledges.

He used the letter with the board, and I heard it had triggered a very large pledge that covered the cost of a new building, which was a major campaign objective. The campaign momentum was then maintained by Ray Carmichael, the college's vice-president for development and a very skilled and knowledgeable fund raiser.

Teachers College had been awarded a Ford Foundation challenge grant, which had to be matched by a specified time—an eventuality I did not see as a realistic expectation. I therefore felt I did not want our firm associated with a campaign that was not going to succeed. Here, too, the termination of our services—and the use that I proposed could be made of it—had a salutary effect on the campaign.

In citing these two instances, I do not mean to give the impression that we believed we should disassociate ourselves from a campaign simply because it was not succeeding. My partners and I felt an obligation to counsel a campaign as long as our services were contributing productively. It was our judgment that we were not being effective and that by resigning, we were making the most forceful statement we could to the boards of these institutions.

The Federation of Protestant Welfare Agencies called us in to do a feasibility study. It was going to be 50 years old and wanted to know if it could raise $50 million in connection with that anniversary's observance.

The Federation was eager to have the study launched, and we started it before we really had a handle on it. Before three weeks went by, I asked to meet with the Federation's development committee and urged that the study be terminated at that point.

As I explained to the committee, it was already apparent that $50 million was not a realistic goal, that those who could give the most would have to reduce their substantial annual support, that annual giving was what should be increased greatly, and that the present endowment had given prospective annual donors the impression that the Federation didn't need further financial support.

The Committee concurred and asked me to provide some initial guidance to the staff in making its annual giving effort more effective. I readily agreed.

Barnes had known Robert P. Roche when they had both previously worked for the John Rich firm in Philadelphia. In 1968, Roche had just finished directing a $93 million capital campaign for the University of Pennsylvania which had raised $103 million. Having achieved that success, he wanted a change and a new challenge. We offered him a full partnership, the inclusion of his name in the firm's name, and (at his request) an office in Philadelphia. The firm's name was changed to Bowen, Gurin, Barnes & Roche, Inc.

And the following year, basically at Roche's initiative, we invited Edmund A. Carlson to become a full member and agreed to open an office for him in Los Angeles. Roche had known Carlson, who had worked in Penn's development department, and during the past year, as a partner of the firm, Roche had counseled him when he was vice-president for development for Loyola University and Marymount College in Los Angeles. And so the firm's name was changed to Bowen, Gurin, Barnes, Roche & Carlson, Inc.

With each of our name changes, the printers profited, for we had to order new stationery. And with each name change, the American Association of Fund-Raising Counsel, Inc., the trade association to which our firm belonged, had to revise its membership directory and other printed literature that listed the member firms. We were a trial and expense to the AAFRC.

47

With the addition of three full partners, the firm took on a less personal and more business like aspect. It had to, for by 1969 we had three offices in different parts of the country, an average of 50 clients a year, and gross annual income in excess of $400,000.

Throughout the 1960s, I represented our firm at meetings of the American Association of Fund-Raising Counsel. I was active in its affairs; and, while I did not agree with all member firms on all matters, I firmly believed in its value for the firms in general and for the practice of fund raising.

There were very estimable gentlemen heading member firms in those years—men like Carlton G. Ketchum and Carl A. Kersting who, by their dedication and leadership, showed that they considered fund raising a calling. And there were younger men, some of them second-generation fund raisers in their families, with impressive credentials. I valued my association with them.

Jim Bryant left the United Negro College Fund to become a program advisor to the Ford Foundation, which had given generous support to predominantly black colleges. In 1970 he invited me to lunch with James W. Armsey, his immediate superior, who during his Foundation career made awards totaling nearly $500 million (mainly matching challenge grants to colleges and universities).

The foundation was interested in assisting black colleges in raising greatly increased funds and, therefore, in alleviating their critical shortage of fund raisers capable of planning and implementing fund-raising campaigns. The question they put forthrightly to me was, "How can we train black fund raisers for the predominantly black colleges?"

I frankly acknowledged that I didn't have a ready answer but I said I thought I could come up with one. As we talked, an approach formed in my mind: our firm would plan and sponsor an all-day conference to formulate an effective training program; we would invite as participants, in addition to our firm's senior professionals, the vice presidents and directors of development of colleges which had effective fund-raising programs.

The proposal appealed to both of them, and Armsey offered to have the Ford Foundation defray the cost of the conference. I declined, saying that I thought we would like to contribute to the program, as well as to volunteer our services. I must confess it was an exhilarating experience to turn down an offer of funds from a foundation whose assets then totaled more than $3 billion.

The conference participants, our firm's professional staff and development officers from some of the most prestigious colleges in the country, appreciated the opportunity to contribute their services. The program formulated at the conference combined on-the-job training (in the development departments of the colleges represented at the conference) with formal education (seminars sponsored by the Ford Foundation to provide the program interns with lectures on the various aspects of fund raising by experienced practitioners).

Armsey and Bryant completely accepted the proposal I submitted which outlined this program. (Armsey conferred an additional accolade on it by saying, "It was in English, too"—from which I assumed that many proposals received by the foundation were not.)

The foundation funded the program, which Bryant administered. He was assisted by a volunteer advisory committee which I had proposed and which consisted of a number of the conference participants: representatives of the participating colleges and associations of professional fund raisers.

Each trainee was to be selected by the president of his college, and all of the predominantly black colleges were invited to identify and propose qualified trainees. To my personal disappointment, nowhere near all of them did. There were 10 trainees the first year and, as I recall, the number was never larger. It seemed to me that greater numbers should have been able to take advantage of this unusual opportunity for both their personal development and the financial advancement of their institutions.

One measure of the program's success was that not all the interns returned to their colleges; some of them were hired away by top-ranking universities eager to engage trained black fund raisers.

The program, subsequently administered from Howard University in Washington, D.C., when Bryant moved there, is continuing to this day. Its graduates even formed their own professional society, the Association of Fund Raising Officers (AFRO).

Looking back on this experience, I know I benefited from the opportunity to help formulate and guide such a program. I am convinced more than ever that it is important for professionals in the field also to serve in appropriate situations as volunteers. And I am proud of my partners for their immediate and enthusiastic agreement to sponsor the original conference. What an investment it turned out to be for so relatively small an expenditure!

Some fund raisers tend to give the impression that they know practically everything there is to know about fund raising; they appear to have all the answers. (I'm not sure I haven't been guilty of the same offense on occasion.)

I remember being acutely aware of this tendency in January 1970 at a regional workshop of the National Society of Fund Raisers (as it was then called) at Johns Hopkins University, where I was asked to evaluate the day-long program.

Every speaker addressed his subject with the confidence and certainty of a practitioner of an exact science. If they knew more, I thought, they would know how much more there was to know.

And then, as I listened to the talks, I recalled that Gertrude Stein had once attended Johns Hopkins. So when I was called on to present my critique, I told the story of how, when Miss Stein was on her deathbed, she was supposed to have sat up suddenly and asked, "What is the answer?" Hearing none, she said, "In that case, what is the question?"

I concluded with the suspicion that not only do we fund raisers not have all the answers, but that we may not even be asking the right questions. The observation could have been taken as a put-down by the previous speakers, but they were apparently oblivious to the implication.

Many of the most assured fund raisers, it seemed to me, are the specialists in such fields as direct mail, planned giving, government grants, and corporate and foundation appeals. These fund raisers are what Ed Gemmell would call mechanics—technicians who had learned the nuts and bolts of some aspect of the business but had not advanced beyond that level.

I have talked to fund-raising groups about my concern that too few general practitioners are being developed—individuals who understand and can respond to an organization's total fund-raising needs.

In the main, the answer for specialists who want to broaden their knowledge and skills has to be in the provision of training opportunities on the staffs of organizations, institutions, and counseling firms.

One of the advantages of having partners in the 1960s was the freedom it gave me to take a vacation and the assurance that the clients I was serving could be provided service in my absence. In those years, I traveled by ship to Europe, where I would spend about six weeks traveling, collecting 17th century English oak furniture and antique pewter, and otherwise unwinding from the pressures built up during the year.

I sometimes had opportunities to combine professional interests with pleasures. Hooker, Craigmyle & Company, Ltd. (later Craigmyle & Company, Ltd.), the largest fund-raising counseling firm in England, annually convened its entire professional staff for a conference during the first few days in August, after which all staff members would take their vacations.

Michael Hooker and later James J. L. Bell, who assumed the management of the firm, often invited me to attend the conferences and to participate in their deliberations. Hooker had studied fund-raising techniques in the United States, had modeled his operations after ours to the extent that they fitted in with British law and custom, and was eager to have me report on recent developments in this country.

It was always enjoyable for me to meet with the members of the firm, most of whom had served in the armed forces and, upon retirement, had joined the firm. I had known many like them when I served with the Army Air Force in England during World War II and got on comfortably with them.

I also got to know Richard Maurice, who headed the second largest firm in Britain. Unlike Craigmyle's men, Maurice's solicited prospective donors for pledges. When I once asked him why he didn't use volunteers as solicitors since they had more status, he replied that his men's status equaled that of the prospects they solicited.

The big difference in fund raising between the two countries then was in the tax advantages available to donors. The United States government permitted a donor to take a tax deduction for his gift. In Britain, the government offered a donor a covenant arrangement by which, if the donor pledged to contribute a set amount to a charity for at least seven years, the government would give the charity the tax on the amount of the gift. Thus, the donation elicited a kind of matching gift from the government.

Because of this covenanting arrangement, a British firm usually sought seven-year pledges in a capital campaign, and then helped the client set up procedures for collecting payments on the pledges. Once the pledges were fully paid, the firm offered to undertake a new campaign. (The British tax laws regarding charitable giving have been liberalized in recent years, as Appendix F indicates.)

British firms have planned campaigns for clients which called for raising part of the needed funds in the United States because they assumed that there were Americans who would have an interest in lending their support. On such occasions, the British firms sometimes have arranged for the services of American firms to assist them here.

In 1969, I met in Geneva with H. F. Tecoz, a Swiss banker with an interest in fund raising, who asked me whether our firm was interested in establishing a European office. I said that until European countries offered tax advantages of substantial interest to donors, our firm was not interested in doing business in Europe.

Walter N. Thayer, president of Whitney Communications Corporation, invited me to meet with him in July of 1968 at the suggestion of Charles T. Hesse, development director of The Museum of Modern Art. Mr. Thayer, who had been president of *The New York Herald Tribune*, had raised funds for Eisenhower's presidential campaigns, and was then heading up the fund-raising effort for the Rockefeller gubernatorial campaign.

A trustee of The Museum of Modern Art, he was enlisted by David Rockefeller, the museum's chairman and chairman of Chase Manhattan Bank, and William S. Paley, the museum's president and chairman of the Columbia Broadcasting System, to serve as chairman of a capital campaign the Modern was then contemplating. Mr. Thayer was seeking fund-raising counsel for the campaign and he interviewed me, as well as representatives of other firms.

I can remember that first meeting with Mr. Thayer to this day. It had to be brief because he was unexpectedly scheduled for a conference 10 minutes later. He therefore proposed that, while we would meet again, he would use the few minutes we had to outline for me what the museum had in mind. And then, suddenly, he asked me what our firm's experience had been with the New York Botanical Garden.

"Disastrous," I said, and made no effort to temper that judgment.

He said he understood it had not been that bad, and returned to the previous discussion until he was summoned to the conference. As I was leaving and we shook hands, he said he'd call me for another meeting. Then he added, "I think we can work together."

It was a comment, not a decision. Indeed, before he decided on our firm, he insisted on meeting and talking with all five of its partners. But I have often thought back on our first meeting, when, as I recall, the only thing I said (apart from pleasantries on arriving and departing) was "Disastrous."

As I began to work with him and came to know him, I was not at all surprised that he had not eliminated us from the competition for the assignment by my straightforward acknowledgment of our firm's unfortunate experience.

I found him to be the kind of capital campaign chairman organizations always seek and rarely find. He was knowledgeable, incisive, and hard-working. He gave first-class attention to the campaign; made the hard decisions; set the example, proportionately, in giving; set the pace in soliciting others; and was persuasive in making the case for support.

The campaign goal, after it was decided to forgo expansion of the museum at that time, was $21.5 million. It was not the largest the Modern had ever set; indeed, the previous 30th Anniversary Campaign had a goal of $25 million. But because this 40th Anniversary Campaign was purely for endowment, its $21.5 million goal was not achieved without difficulty.

A footnote to the campaign proved to be of historic interest to the museum. It was a suggestion, made in connection with the feasibility study our firm conducted but unrelated to the study's conventional capital campaign thrust, that the trustees consider the construction of a commercial office tower atop—or adjacent to—the museum as an income-producing property. The Modern owned very valuable air rights appurtenant to its property, which was located in a choice section of mid-town Manhattan, and such an office tower would enable the museum to realize the value of this latent asset.

This suggestion emerged from a conversation that I had with Richard H. Koch, the museum's director of administration and general counsel; it had been advanced by my partners in Philadelphia to the Friends Select School, which (as previously described in this chapter) had acted on it successfully.

The leadership of the museum was taken with the suggestion at the outset. However, because of a number of adverse factors (including the advent of a recession and the diminished demand for office space), the suggestion was shelved. It was not to re-emerge for nearly a decade, and then in a new mode.

54

*   *   *

Frequently, conflicts of interest are viewed differently by a client and a consultant. A client likes to feel that he has the consultant's total attention and commitment, and is not sharing them with another client in the same vicinity.

In the early 1970s, my partners and I held an exploratory talk with Kendall Landis, vice-president for development at Swarthmore College. He was impressed with out firm because we were counseling the University of Pennsylvania and Haverford College, both of which were in the general vicinity.

But what impressed him was also what worried him. He feared that there could be competition for our firm's attention and commitment, and if he engaged our firm, Swarthmore could suffer. He was particularly concerned about the possibility of competition for prospective donors.

We explained that each institution, however closely situated it was to the others, had its own constituency and (assuming it had been kept informed and interested) its allegiance. Certainly the alumni of one would not give its primary support to another.

As for the relatively small number of prospects (friends, corporations, and foundations) which could be approached by all three institutions, each of them would have an appeal based upon its own particular needs and gift opportunities. The one whose needs most closely matched the special interests of the prospects would prevail.

We therefore contended that having Penn and Haverford as clients did not lessen our value for Swarthmore; indeed, because of our knowledge of fund-raising conditions and opportunities in the locale they helped provide, they increased our value for other nearby institutions. Swarthmore became a client.

In the 1960s when we counseled an endowment campaign for the New York Philharmonic, I was asked to meet with an officer of the American Symphony Orchestra which performed at Carnegie Hall. I said I would have to check with Amyas Ames, president of the Philharmonic, on the possibility of a conflict of interest.

Mr. Ames told me that he could discern no conflict of interest. He added, however, that since I seemed to have a concern about it, he would go along with my judgment.

When I was counseling The Museum of Modern Art on its 40th Anniversary Campaign in the late 1960s, our firm was approached by a representative of the Metropolitan Museum of Art. Before pursuing that inquiry, I sought the guidance of William S. Paley, president of the Modern.

I was advised that, because the Metropolitan had recently made a major move into modern art and the two institutions could be competitive, he would appreciate it if we did not follow up on the Met inquiry.

Our clients were our first concern. We respected their wishes and in the absence of their objections, we made it a policy of leaning over backward to assure ourselves that no conflict of interest would result from the addition of a client.

The enlistment of strong fund-raising leadership is usually difficult for any organization—and particularly for one which has never before had to attract broad public support. Such an organization was the National League for Nursing, which for the first 19 years of its existence was able to support itself through its own membership and operations (such as fees for a variety of testing services, which were the most extensive of their kind in the country).

This enviable state ended in 1971 when the League recognized that its internal organizational sources of support were no longer adequate for its needs and that it must appeal for public support. Since fund raising had not previously been a requirement, the membership of the League's board did not include volunteers with fund-raising clout. It therefore had to look for such leadership on the outside.

The only board member I thought could be helpful in this effort was Mrs. Mary Todhunter Rockefeller, and she agreed to help enlist a chairman for the League's newly constituted Committee on Development of Resources.

She suggested Thomas S. Gates, board chairman of Morgan Guaranty Trust Company of New York, whom she knew from years past when she lived on Philadelphia's Main Line. My reaction was that he was first-rate—perhaps too important for the task at hand—but that it was certainly worth trying to enlist him.

Mrs. Rockefeller was delightfully straightforward, and asked me what specifically she should do. I suggested that she broach the idea to Mr. Gates, and ask him not to give an immediate answer and agree to hear more about what the League hoped he would do from its president and general director.

She phoned me soon thereafter to report that she had followed my suggested procedure, that Mr. Gates had agreed to hear more, but that he wanted to speak with me because he thought that I could give him the clearest understanding of what the fund-raising position would entail.

When I called on Mr. Gates at his office, he was equally straightforward. He asked what, exactly, he would be letting himself in for. I answered honestly, making no attempt to portray the position in unrealistic terms.

His major concern, however, did not relate to the work that would be required. He couldn't see how he could be a credible spokesman for nursing. Education? Yes, he had been active on behalf of education. (I knew this because Bob Roche, while still at the University of Pennsylvania, had worked with Mr. Gates who had enlisted volunteer leadership for Penn's $93 million capital campaign.) But nursing? That was not a field in which he had—or was recognized as having—a personal concern.

His observation was well taken, and I felt it would serve no useful purpose to do anything but acquiesce in his judgment that he was not appropriate for the fund-raising role the League hoped he would accept. Indeed, I recognized that Mr. Gates had stated a sound development requirement: a volunteer fund-raising leader should be perceived as one who is—and could be expected to be—personally committed to the cause he espouses.

A national voluntary health organization can benefit greatly from an objective reading on the statement of the case for the cause

it advances. Certainly communicating the case clearly is important. Perhaps even more important is the accuracy and complete-
ness of the statement.

Unless the case statement is accurate and complete (neither
exaggerated nor understated), the public could be misled, patients
could be misinformed, and physicians generally could be under
some misapprehensions. As a result, the organization's program
and support could suffer.

The development that focused the attention of the American
Diabetes Association on its case in 1969 was the interest of the
organization, which had been basically a professional society and
was converting to a voluntary health agency, in undertaking a
national fund-raising campaign. Our firm was engaged to determine through a study when the ADA would be capable of conducting such a campaign, and our study's findings disclosed the weak-
ness of the organization's case for diabetes.

We found that the perception of diabetes as a health problem
reflected the ADA's public statement of the case, which depicted
diabetes generally as a condition that, if detected early, was
usually manageable with medical care and diet control. The statement, and consequently the organization, referred to diabetes as
an ailment or affliction, as well as a condition; it did not term
diabetes a disease.

Upon our recommendation, the ADA board moved promptly to
strengthen the case. It approved a new statement that described
diabetes as a major health problem, one that contributes to many
other health problems and may significantly decrease life
expectancy.

The statement noted that complications occur frequently despite treatment with diet, insulin, or oral drugs. For children and
adolescents, impairment of vision is a frequent complication, life
expectancy is shortened, and the most common cause of death is
diabetic kidney disease. For those in middle age, the most common
complication is hardening of the arteries with subsequent heart
attack, stroke, or gangrene.

In this country, the statement observed, diabetes is ranked as
the fifth leading cause of death by disease and the second leading

cause of blindness; heart attacks are two-and-a-half times more frequent in diabetics than in nondiabetics of the same age.

This realistic statement was important programmatically. Patients have a right to know the full implications of their disease; in fact, if they don't know its seriousness, they could very well neglect it. The public has an interest to know because many Americans could have diabetes and not know it; and if they are not properly informed, they might not pay adequate attention to early symptoms of the disease.

This realistic statement was also important for fund raising. At last, as J. Richard Connelly, ADA's executive director, noted, the organization could produce fund-raising material that could tug at the heart—and the purse strings—and that could give the facts to rationalize the emotional urge to contribute.

The ADA faced another problem that significantly affected its organizational development. Many diabetics did not want to affiliate with the ADA (and thus assist it in furthering the cause which should be closest to their hearts), because they were ashamed to have it known that they had diabetes.

With this problem, it seemed to me, physicians could be most helpful. While it is not the usual role of a fund-raising consultant to address the medical leadership of a national voluntary health organization, Connelly arranged for me to have that opportunity.

I held that physicians treating diabetics had an interest in helping to change their attitude about diabetes; that it was "healthy" for diabetics to face up to their condition and not feel embarrassed by it; and that, as a result, they would be more likely to take better care of themselves. With such a healthy attitude, I noted, diabetics would feel free to join the ADA membership and help advance the care and ultimate cure of their disease.

I cannot recall a role I ever played that gave me greater personal satisfaction. But this was not the only opportunity that Connelly made available to me; he also scheduled me as a speaker at the ADA's annual meeting.

Having worked so closely and congenially with Connelly, I was not displeased that the conclusion of my arrangement with the organization coincided with the termination of his services as executive director, a position he had filled since the ADA was founded more than a quarter of a century before.

While I was directing a fund-raising study for Wesleyan University at Middletown, Connecticut, in 1969, I happened to hear a story about a previous effort by the university to undertake a capital campaign that was both delightful and instructive. It concerned John E. Andrus, one of the university's most generous alumni, who founded the Surdna (Andrus spelled backward) Foundation with assets well over $100 million.

He was on one of his periodic visits to the campus when the administration was starting to plan a capital campaign for $6 million (a goal that by its modest size indicates how long ago that was). Hearing of the contemplated campaign, he approved of it to the extent that he sat down and wrote out a check for the full amount of the goal.

His generosity completed the campaign before it was even launched. If there is a moral to this story, I think it is that a capital campaign should seek to meet the immediate objectives of a longer-term development program, and that less urgent objectives of the program (assuming they cannot be achieved in the traditional campaign period) should also be exposed to major prospects.

If that had been done, Mr. Andrus could have been told that his generosity had enabled Wesleyan to complete phase one of its development program and launch phase two.

Wesleyan's endowment in 1969 was $170 million—the largest per student of any university in the country. But, as we learned in the study, that endowment was in no way an indication of the constituency's giving potential. It came from the sale of the university's American Education Publications to the Xerox Corporation, and grew when the Xerox stock the university received in payment appreciated in value.

The constituency had very limited financial resources. The university turned out graduates who, for the most part, entered such occupations as teaching and the ministry. Relatively few alumni earned or inherited substantial wealth.

These findings called into question the appropriateness of the traditional capital campaign, since too small a percentage of the university's total needs of $57 million could be raised in such a campaign. We proposed instead a 10-year development program for $40 million (should hard-core objectives require such a goal) that was specifically tailored to the financial capabilities of the university's constituency.

Through this program, professional estate planning assistance would be offered to all capital gift prospects to enable them to determine how they could make their finest commitments. In addition, annual giving would be developed to the utmost to attract increasing annual support, encourage bequests to perpetuate lifetime giving, and identify additional prospects for capital gifts.

Our study was made during the presidency of Edwin D. Etherington, who had formerly headed the American Stock Exchange. The presidents of several other universities had been enlisted for Wesleyan's board, and I remember thinking that if any of them helped raise funds for Wesleyan, they could be in trouble with their own boards.

Our firm's contracts to conduct a study never obligated a client to use our services for any subsequent capital campaign that might be indicated, and Wesleyan did not engage us to counsel the capital development program we proposed.

Over and above what it raised for its own program, the Arthritis Foundation in 1965 was interested in providing for the continuing support of a network of 17 clinical research centers it "inherited" from the National Foundation/March of Dimes.

When polio ceased to be a health problem in the late 1950s, the National Foundation for Infantile Paralysis changed its name to the National Foundation and focused on arthritis and birth defects. It initiated merger talks with the Arthritis Foundation (then called the Arthritis and Rheumatism Foundation), a much smaller voluntary health organization.

The talks failed and the National Foundation decided to relinquish arthritis to the Arthritis Foundation, which took over the clinical research centers. Dr. William S. Clark, who had presided over the organization of the centers, became the president of the Arthritis Foundation.

It was Dr. Clark who engaged our firm to determine whether the organization could raise $1.5 million in a special gift campaign over a three-year period to meet the capital needs for continuing the program of the clinical research centers.

Through the fund-raising survey we conducted, we found that a nationally directed capital campaign for the desired goal was neither practical nor advisable. We therefore explored alternatives to a capital campaign.

The alternative we recommended called for the foundation to ask the chapters in the vicinity of 15 centers to support them as local projects, and to form chapters in the two cities where centers were located and no chapters existed.

We noted that local special gifts solicitations undertaken by the chapters could be conducted with the assistance of the national organization's enlarged field staff. Such a staff would preclude the need for further assistance from a counseling firm.

# 3

# Doing Individual Consulting

And then the ties that bound Bowen, Gurin, Barnes, Roche & Carlson, Inc. began to unravel. Bowen and I became critical of Carlson for not signing more clients and for the Los Angeles office's drain on the firm's finances. Later, the number of clients that Bowen was handling dwindled, and Carlson became critical of Bowen's diminished contribution to the firm's business.

Our corporate name began to shrink.

Bowen, sensitive to the situation, left to join the Brakeley, John Price Jones firm as a senior vice president; accordingly, our firm name was changed to Gurin, Barnes, Roche & Carlson, Inc. Subsequently, as a result of a serious difference among the partners over counseling practice, Carlson left the firm. The departure of a second partner required another change in the name of our firm, which then became Gurin, Barnes & Roche, Inc.

But even after the closing of the Los Angeles office that Carlson had run, the firm was still too large for me really to know what the Philadelphia office was doing, or Barnes and Roche to know what I was doing in the New York office. While the three of us were very busy serving clients, we certainly could have maintained an integrated firm if we had had the inclination to keep each other informed.

Apparently that inclination was not present. I therefore proposed that each office, with the clients it was then serving, go its separate way. Barnes and Roche accepted the proposal with alacrity.

\*    \*    \*

And so in October 1972, after a 14-year immersion in the hectic business of building a nationwide counseling firm by the accretion of partners, I was back under my own—my completely own—banner. The banner I chose was The Gurin Group, Inc. For whatever—if any—distinction it may represent, it was the first use made of the term "group" to designate a fund-raising counseling firm.

Its choice was determined by alliteration (I thought "group" sounded good with "Gurin") and by allergic reaction to the standard designations: "associates" (used by so many firms) and "company" (used more appropriately by industrial and commercial concerns).

It was a heady feeling to be completely free of previous constraints, to be able to make decisions without consultation, to act on one's own priorities and preferences. And yet, as much as I felt profound relief at being free of partners, I confess that if I had to do it all over again, I would probably have taken the same route in building a large firm.

The usual alternative, a sole proprietorship, would not have seemed preferable. Such a firm can grow by adding employees. But when some of them develop their full potential and are not made partners, they become restless and are difficult, if not impossible, to retain.

I also admit that if I had not had partners, I would not have experienced the urge to build a sizeable firm. I doubt that I would have felt the impulse on my own; I would probably have been content to stay small and comfortable, untroubled by the exertion and pains of growth.


The many and frequent changes in the corporate name of the firm I served as president were a source of occasional confusion and frequent amusement to clients, colleagues, and friends. Once, to see how it looked, I listed the various changes under the heading, "Corporate Evolution":

Bowen & Gurin, Inc.
Bowen & Gurin & Barnes, Inc.
Bowen, Gurin, Barnes & Roche, Inc.
Bowen, Gurin, Barnes, Roche & Carlson, Inc.
Gurin, Barnes, Roche & Carlson, Inc.
Gurin, Barnes & Roche, Inc.
The Gurin Group, Inc.

It seemed amusing to me, and I had the typed sheet framed and mounted on my office wall. Mrs. Flora Irving, president of the Whitney Museum of American Art and granddaughter of its founder, was in my office some time later and noticed the "Corporate Evolution." "It's diamond-shaped," she said, stopping short of calling it a work of art.

The Gurin Group, Inc. was welcomed as a member of the American Association of Fund-Raising Counsel. (Barnes & Roche, Inc., the firm my former partners formed, did not apply for continued membership.)

The Gurin Group, Inc. sounds like it encompasses impressive numbers. Actually, when it was formed, I had with me only Sarah Jesup and a secretary, since all my former colleagues had been working out of the Philadelphia office. But Sarah and I had little difficulty in serving our clients.

In the first year, our clients included the American Diabetes Association, American Field Service, the Asia Society, CARE, Greenwich Academy, Lenox School, The Museum of Modern Art, the National Foundation for Infectious Diseases, the National Foundation for Ileitis & Colitis, and WNET/Channel 13.

Sarah had joined our firm several years before and, at her own insistence, started as a secretary. But before long she took over the management of the office. The only training she had as a fund raiser was in assisting me in the conduct of several feasibility studies (and, incidentally, I don't know of a better or quicker way to learn about a capital campaign than to participate in the conduct of a study and, if the goal is feasible, in the formulation of a campaign plan to achieve the goal).

What I was not aware of was all that she was doing on her own. She must have absorbed everything that was said in the office and everything that was prepared for clients. But I did know she was becoming increasingly intrigued by fund raising and enthusiastic about being in the business. I saw that she could develop into a first-rate consultant, and I awaited an appropriate client for her.

The Greenwich Academy, a highly rated girls secondary school, asked to see us about a capital campaign it was planning. Sarah drove me to Greenwich along the Connecticut coast; en route, I said, "If we are engaged to counsel the school, I think you should take on the assignment."

"Do you think I am ready for that?" she asked.

"You can do it," I assured her. "And besides, I'll always be available if you need me."

That was the last time she indicated any doubt about her readiness. We got the assignment, she was readily accepted as the consultant by the administration and the volunteer leadership, and she never did call on me for advice. Not that she didn't encounter problems—practically every capital campaign has problems—but she confronted them squarely and resolved them.

She was attractive, competent, and enthusiastic, and the volunteers in the campaign organization enjoyed working with her. She had been a volunteer fund raiser when she was married and living in Bristol, Connecticut, and she therefore knew how to relate to volunteers. Most of all, she was a genuinely decent human being. That may sound old-fashioned and unsophisticated, but I think it counts importantly in fund raising.

I often would bring Sarah along when I attended meetings of the American Association of Fund-Raising Counsel. While one or two other women occasionally were present, they were not functioning as consultants. A woman in that role was still something new for firms.

Some firms wondered what a client's reactions might be to a woman consultant. When I wanted to involve Sarah in an assignment, I never asked the client; I simply brought her along. When I next saw the client alone, I was usually asked why she hadn't come. I never anticipated a problem, and with Sarah there never was one.

\*  \*  \*

The Asia Society in the summer of 1973 was interested in learning whether it could undertake a campaign for a larger headquarters building. The Society was founded 17 years before by John D. Rockefeller 3rd, who had previously revived the Japan Society. The Asia Society's program, while it included Japan, encompassed all of the Asian countries.

Asia House, the Society's national headquarters, was inadequate to accommodate its expanded program and enlarged professional staff, some of whom had to be housed in outside facilities. Its inadequacy would also keep the Society from taking advantage of an unusual opportunity it was anticipating: an offer by its founder of his and Mrs. Rockefeller's Asian art collection, which was estimated to be worth between $10 and $15 million.

The audit I was commissioned to make by Phillips Talbot, the Society's president, gave the board the assurance that it could embark upon a capital campaign for a larger building. But the audit also indicated the need to strengthen the board for campaign purposes by the addition of other individuals who, besides being interested in the Society's program, could give and ask for the very substantial capital commitments that were required to achieve the campaign goal (which, when it was firmed up, totaled $19.75 million).

The only objection to more members was a preference for a "small, working board." It was my view that there was no such thing as a "working board" since a board had no time to work and therefore could only pass on the work done by committees—to approve or disapprove committee recommendations, or to refer recommendations back to committee for further consideration.

But then the need for a substantially strengthened board became painfully clear: Mr. Rockefeller lost his life in a tragic automobile accident.

The loss that his death represented to the Asia Society was severe indeed. It moved the board to increase its numbers and thus try to compensate for all that Mr. Rockefeller had meant to the Society in leadership and support.

The new and larger Asia House in New York City, which opened its doors in April 1981, is in a very real sense a monument to Mr.

Rockefeller, as is Lincoln Center for the Performing Arts, for which he also was largely responsible.

America's inadequate understanding of Asia and Asians was one of Mr. Rockefeller's major concerns. He once expressed that concern in one sentence, which was a powerful statement of the case for the Asia Society's program: "After being involved in three land wars in Asia in one generation, we Americans must seek afresh to develop understanding and cooperation with two-thirds of the human family who live in Asia."

The Asia Society's campaign chairman, whose role is always central, was ably filled by G. A. Constanzo, vice chairman of Citicorp, who gave it his unrelenting attention. His solicitation of corporate commitments was particularly impressive. Indeed, his personal calls on major out-of-state corporate prospects obviously impressed them with his own commitment to the campaign and his conviction of its importance.

Early in 1974, Walter Thayer asked me to meet with several officials of Eisenhower College to review its fund-raising program and make any suggestions I might think could be helpful. I was happy to oblige, and in the process I learned something of his activities in behalf of the college, which opened in 1965 in Seneca Falls, New York.

Eisenhower College was founded by friends and colleagues of the former president as a four-year liberal arts institution. It was financed by private funds and federal grants totaling $14.5 million. But it experienced financial difficulties almost from the start.

A campaign for private funds did not attain its goal; Congress blocked an effort, developed by Mr. Thayer, to give the college $1 for every special proof edition of the Eisenhower silver dollars that were to be minted and sold by the U.S Treasury Department.

When the trustees thought they might have to close the college in 1974, the New York State Legislature came to its rescue with a $2 million loan. Then Congress made an $8.1 million grant to the college and approved the Eisenhower coin proposal. This Congressional support was attributable in large measure to Mr. Thayer's persuasion and persistence.

Such sums are not impressive, however, in terms of the far greater financial needs that a college—let alone a new one situated in a remote location—requires for its survival, if not for excellence. And so in 1979, the Rochester Institute of Technology undertook to operate Eisenhower College as one of its 10 constituent colleges.

Financial difficulties persisted and after losing $5.7 million in three years, the college was closed by the Institute in July 1982 because of "a declining pool of college-age students, cutbacks in federal aid, and the inability to attract sufficient financial support."

It was ironic that the college closed, leaving no memorial to Dwight David Eisenhower, at the very time when his presidency was being critically upgraded and accorded greater recognition.

There is a fairly widespread view among volunteer leaders of nonprofit organizations that a professional fund-raising study to test the feasibility of a projected campaign goal always comes up with an affirmative result. In this view, a study is only a preliminary exercise for a fund-raising firm to undertake for the purpose of recommending—and counseling—a campaign.

I cannot deny that a study is a necessary preliminary to a campaign or that a firm undertaking a study hopes it will lead to a campaign. But I cannot conceive how a firm, learning through a study that a projected goal is unrealistic, would want to recommend a campaign or would want to be associated as counsel with a campaign doomed to failure.

It is certainly not a pleasant experience for fund-raising counsel, as I can attest, to have to tell an organization intent on raising an ambitious goal to fund a worthwhile objective that it cannot expect to succeed in such an undertaking. But counsel at least can take comfort in the knowledge that he has discouraged the organization from embarking upon an expensive no-win enterprise.

Such an organization was the National Foundation for Infectious Diseases (NFID). In 1973, The Gurin Group, Inc. was retained to plan and conduct a study of the newly formed agency's fund-raising potential. In the study, Sarah Jesup and I tested the feasibility of raising annual funds at an initial level of $7,675,000.

We found conclusive evidence that such a fund-raising expectation was completely unrealistic. The NFID's major problem was its inclusion of about 50 infectious diseases under its organizational umbrella.

We questioned whether any organization, whatever its structural strength and financial resources, could deal effectively with so many disease entities. We could see how the NFID could duplicate the work of a number of other national voluntary health agencies in specific disease areas which have well-established organizational structures and sources of support.

The number of varying causal factors of the diseases militated against the likelihood that the NFID would be able to mount a single medical, educational, and/or research approach. As a result, there didn't seem to be any advantage in dealing with these diseases as a group.

From what we were able to learn, the public did not envisage infectious diseases as a separate health cause, and individuals could not identify with it significantly. The grouping of these diseases, therefore, did not provide fund-raising appeal.

Even with findings as negative as these, fund-raising counsel cannot just say to the committed and concerned leaders of a health organization: "Forget it." We urged the leaders of the NFID to go back to the drawing board. We proposed that they re-evaluate their program and structure in light of our findings.

Our study report was accepted by the NFID's board. But I never heard whether it acted on our proposal and, if it did, whether it was able to fashion a more manageable and practical vehicle to advance its objectives.

We conducted a number of fund-raising studies which indicated a campaign could be undertaken but which did not recommend fund-raising counsel. One such study, commissioned by the Parkinson's Disease Foundation, was made to assist the organization in determining how to strengthen its program, structure, and support.

Our recommendations did not include counseling service, for we believed that the foundation could be adequately assisted in its fund raising by the addition to its staff of an effective director of development. This recommendation was in keeping with our policy to propose counseling service only when we were needed to augment staff capabilities.

What was unusual for us was to have to recommend that the board be given full voice in decision making. The one board meeting I subsequently attended confirmed the validity of that recommendation: the few board members who tried to voice their opinions were frequently cut off by the chairman, William Black.

While not physically impressive, he had a commanding personality and dominated the meeting. He interrupted me often during the course of my oral report to the board. Because I had seen the board members intimidated by him, I did not give an inch on a number of questions he asked about the study report. Indeed, I said he would not have had to ask most of the questions if he had participated in the study, which he had refused to do, telling me he could not spare the time.

I remember feeling so irritated that, when the questioning of the study report concluded, I picked up my papers, left the room, and headed for the elevator (which was on the 20th floor of the William Black Medical Research Building at Columbia University's College of Physicians and Surgeons). I heard footsteps behind me and, turning, saw that Mr. Black had followed me.

"I want you to understand. . ." he started to say, but the elevator had come and I interrupted him.

"I'm sorry but I have another appointment," I said and entered the elevator. He followed me in and took me by the arm.

"I want you to understand," he continued, "that the only reason I talk so much is that the others never say anything."

"Mr. Black," I said, "you interrupted every board member who tried to speak."

He switched the subject to the wealthiest member of the board. "He should give more than I give," he said.

"That may be," I said, "but I understand that you refuse to ask others to give."

"I'll do it," he said. "I'll ask him."

"I'll keep you to that promise," I said.

We had arrived at the lobby floor. He was still trying to convince me that my impression of him was wrong. I could only assume he was interested because I stood up to him. But by now I was aware that my irritation with him had evaporated and had been replaced by a grudging admiration.

"I'll say this for you, Mr. Black, you put your hand where your mouth is." And I patted him affectionately on the back and left.

Like many fund raisers, I can forgive much in one who gives generously. He was the largest donor to the foundation, which had the 20th floor of the building as its headquarters. (He had insisted on that arrangement at the time of his $5 million gift to the university toward the building that would bear his name.)

He founded the Parkinson's Disease Foundation to advance research when a business associate and lifelong friend died from the disease. In addition to money, he contributed ideas—even scientific ideas. One of them—to use primates in the research program—was scoffed at initially by the foundation's scientific advisors but was ultimately found to have value and was acted on.

At the time of our study in mid-1970, I read that the business he built—Chock Full o'Nuts Corporation—was doing about $60 million a year. Yet when I had phoned him for an appointment to participate in the study and had asked for his secretary, I was told that he had none and was connected directly to him.

But there was nothing frugal about William Black when it came to philanthropy. In addition to his $5 million gift to Columbia (then the largest contribution ever made by a living person to the university), he made major gifts to the Mount Sinai School of Medicine and the Lenox Hill Hospital's Nursing School.

It was my impression that, among the major donors to medical education, medical research, and nursing in New York, he gave more than most in proportion to his means.

72

\*   \*   \*

Sarah Jesup left the firm to become director of development and alumni affairs of the Collegiate School in New York, the oldest independent school in the country. From the move she gained a substantial salary increase, permission to accept additional fund-raising assignments, and waiver of tuition for her sons Randell and Benjamin.

For the first time in her fund-raising career, she was out from under my shadow and she really came into her own. She worked well in tandem with Dr. Richard Barter, the headmaster, and was warmly regarded and highly respected by the faculty and the parents.

One of the first development requirements (apart from the need for increased annual giving) she faced was to raise several million dollars in capital funds. For the pre-campaign feasibility study, she selected the Brakeley, John Price Jones firm, and the study was conducted by Lew Bowen. She didn't ask me to bid for the study, assuming (I believe) that if she called me, it would look as if she had not made an unbiased decision.

While she must have known that I would have been glad to offer her any advice she might need, she made a point of practically never asking me for any professional guidance. She began to invite me to social events, such as the annual theater benefit of the Bryn Mawr Club of New York, of which she was president. We changed from colleagues to friends.

Suddenly, in 1976, when she was only in her 41st year and when all was going so well with her, she developed cancer of the breast. When she first went to her doctor, she said he told her it was nothing to be concerned about. When she returned to him some time later, he rushed her to the hospital for a mastectomy. With characteristic courage and good cheer, she endured several other operations—all designed to halt the spread of cancer. They all failed.

During the period when she was being treated with chemo-therapy at Memorial Hospital for Cancer and Allied Diseases, she told me that she liked her oncologist because he did not try to kid her into thinking all would be well. She broke up over his remark that she transferred from Presbyterian Hospital (located on the upper West Side of Manhattan) to Memorial because she wanted to die on the fashionable East Side.

Because her medical expenses became a problem, she needed to increase her income. Fortunately, Lisa Pulling, executive director of The Fresh Air Fund, asked her to serve as fund-raising counsel to the Fund's 100th anniversary capital campaign for $2 million. To save Sarah the trouble of registering as an independent consultant, I agreed to handle the Fund as my firm's client. I billed the Fund for the monthly counseling fee she earned, and sent her the money.

We would meet for dinner occasionally. She always ordered sweetbreads, for which I never acquired a taste. She almost never mentioned her medical condition, and I was hesitant to ask about it. When I left her at her apartment the last time I saw her, she said I was "such a comfort" to her. I felt so stupidly helpless, I couldn't make any response.

And then, mercifully, and more quickly than expected, the end came. The West End Collegiate Church, where the memorial services were held, was completely filled. Many of those in attendance, I noticed, were friends of hers who knew each other through her; she had brought them together.

The services were so understated and impersonal that I remember wishing that someone would stand up and just say, "We all think Sarah was wonderful and we will miss her." I confess I wanted to—and couldn't.

I phoned Lisa Pulling some days later to advise that, since Sarah was gone, I was terminating The Fresh Air Fund as a client. She responded by asking whether I could meet her that afternoon on a problem that had arisen. That meeting was followed by many others and I became the firm's consultant to the capital campaign, which was then about $500,000 short of its goal.

Arthur Ochs Sulzberger, publisher of *The New York Times*, was campaign chairman, and the campaign committee would meet periodically in the *Times'* board room. Mr. Sulzberger not only committed the *Times* to publicize and promote the campaign, he also accounted for the largest pledge and solicited many prospective donors.

He once asked whether it would be helpful to run a full-page ad appealing for additional corporate contributions. I said it was certainly generous of him to make the offer, but I thought he would be disappointed in the results.

I noted, however, that he could run an ad to thank the 30-some corporations which had already contributed; that such an ad would be justified in terms of donor recognition; and that it could serve to attract other corporate donors—particularly if there were to be subsequent ads. With customary generosity, he accepted the idea.

The ad appeared—and it produced the desired effect. Amory Houghton, Jr., board chairman of Corning Glass (one of the companies listed in the ad), mentioned to his wife, a member of the Fresh Air Fund board, that he was amazed at how many other corporate executives noticed Corning Glass in the ad and had phoned to congratulate him.

At the request of his wife, who had accounted for many of the corporate contributors listed in the ad, Mr. Houghton sent a letter to the executives who had congratulated him and urged them to make their corporate contributions and be listed in the next *New York Times* ad. He was responsible for eight more corporations being added to the list.

But a capital campaign for $2 million in endowment could not meet all of the Fund's financial needs in the immediate years ahead, for they would far exceed any income this endowment could generate. What was urgently required, in my view, was increased effectiveness in attracting annual contributions through a structured approach.

Traditionally, annual gift support had been sought in a rather loose and unorganized way, with only a few board members and the executive director making any fund-raising approaches other than by mail appeal. In 1978, Mr. Sulzberger, who had been elected chairman of the Fund, acted on my suggestion and designated an annual giving committee. The benefits that resulted from that action were measurable.

In 1977, the year before an annual giving committee was formed, the Fund had raised $946,576. By 1982, it had raised $1,570,000. Thus, in five years, the committee had increased the Fund's annual support by more than 50 percent. In addition, in 1982, while most gift-supported organizations were striving to survive a depressed economy and the Reagan administration cutbacks, the Fund increased its annual support by 11 percent over the previous year's receipts.

A productive idea sparked in conference with Mr. Sulzberger was to undertake a professionally guided self-study of the Fund. The purpose of the study, as it was envisioned, was to learn whether the Fund's program, which had been initiated in the 19th century, was currently relevant and responsive to the needs of the city's underprivileged children.

The most positive finding of the study was that the Fund's program not only had health and recreational benefits for the children it served, it also had important educational and cultural values for them.

In terms of their aspirations for the future, the children interviewed in the study showed they were committed to a better life: 50 percent of them hoped for a professional or managerial position, and 78 percent wanted to go to college. An even higher proportion—84 percent—of their parents hoped their children would get a college education.

To kindle such aspirations represented a wholly new and meaningful dimension for a program that had previously promised only a two-week vacation in the country.

John Temple Swing, vice president of the Council on Foreign Relations, heard about me in 1978 from Dick Koch. The Council, which drew most of its financial support from its 1,800 members, had initiated a $10 million capital campaign, which for some months had plateaued at $5.5 million.

It was my judgment that, since the goal had not been tested in a feasibility study, it could well be unrealistic. In addition, because of the strength of the campaign leadership (which included David Rockefeller, board chairman, and C. Douglas Dillon, vice chairman), the funds that had been raised could be considerably more than could ordinarily have been obtained.

I therefore recommended against trying to revive the campaign and urged instead that the organization concentrate on strengthening its annual giving program. My advice was accepted and annual giving was invigorated by John D. Macomber, president of the Celanese Corporation, who was appointed chairman of the program.

The professional fund-raising responsibility at the Council had been divided among several staff members, for whom it had been an additional duty. I recommended that a director of development be engaged to assume full fund-raising responsibility; this was done. And so, after I set the basic fund-raising directions, there was no longer need for my services.

WNET/Channel 13 was preparing to embark upon a $10 million Ford Foundation matching challenge campaign; at Ed Gemmell's suggestion, I met with Hudson G. Stoddard, vice president for development, and was engaged as consultant to the campaign.

The Ford Foundation, in phasing down its annual support of public television, had pledged to pay WNET/Channel 13 this terminal grant over the next five years provided the station raised an equal amount from the community.

Public television was a relatively new cause for philanthropic support in 1973; the station was then only 10 years old. It certainly represented for us a different kind of client for a capital campaign. Whether it had among its viewers sufficient donors capable of making the level of capital gifts needed in such a campaign was something to be determined by the campaign itself, for the station did not authorize a feasibility study.

A distinguishing feature about this client that interested me from the outset was that it had its own built-in communications medium to promote the campaign. What an asset that could be, I thought. One of my first campaign memoranda listed a number of ways in which the campaign could be advanced "on air" by Channel 13.

The campaign succeeded—and, indeed, exceeded its $10 million goal by $3.5 million. But ironically, the station made practically no use of its own medium for reaching the general viewing public or specific types of prospective donors in the public.

The campaign succeeded because of strong volunteer leadership. Ethan Allen Hitchcock, chairman of the station's board, also assumed the campaign chairmanship. He gave it dedication and first-class attention, he made the important solicitations, and he had the courage to ask for the large amounts.

Typical was his solicitation of Thomas Mellon Evans, who had been a classmate of his many years before at Yale University. The campaign was seeking leadership pledges of $100,000 or more, and one day Mr. Hitchcock mentioned that he thought he would call on Mr. Evans and ask him for a pledge in that amount.

Since Mr. Evans had not been a prospect previously and had not been cultivated, my immediate reaction ordinarily would have been to urge that the solicitation be put off until such time as his interest was ascertained and his readiness to pledge generously was indicated. But some second sense restrained me.

Mr. Hitchcock made the solicitation call and returned with a pledge of $100,000. And later, encouraged by the pledge, he decided to learn whether Mr. Evans would be interested in making a far greater gift and putting his name on the building.

That raised a complication, for the station's new home was being constructed in the first eight floors of the Henry Hudson Hotel. Subsequently, Mr. Hitchcock phoned to say that Mr. Evans had asked about the length of the station's lease with the hotel. I suggested that Mr. Evans be assured that if the station ever moved, any plaque with his name on it would move with the station.

Mr. Hitchcock forged an effective campaign team with John Jay Iselin, station president, and Hud Stoddard. He was instrumental in strengthening the board with such influential new directors as Mrs. Brooke Astor and Mrs. Jane Engelhard.

The campaign's success—representing by far the largest capital campaign goal achieved by any public television station in the country—enabled Channel 13 to create the premier broadcast and production center for public television in the United States.

The fulcrum of The Museum of Modern Art's 50th Anniversary Program, which provided the leverage for the $75 million capital campaign it encompassed, was the concept of constructing a condominium apartment tower atop a new west wing of the museum to realize the income-producing potential of its frozen air rights.

This concept represented the re-emergence in revised form of the suggestion made to the museum trustees in 1968 about construction of a commercial office tower above the Modern. The concept owed its attraction to the success of the nearby Olympic Tower and to the demand for condominium apartments in 1977, when the Modern's program was launched.

Conceptually, the program was the joint product of Richard H. Koch, the museum official who had suggested the program in its earlier form; Richard S. Weinstein, former director of the Mayor's Office for Planning and Development for Lower Manhattan; and Donald H. Elliott, former chairman of the New York City Planning Commission.

The development program, which included the most ambitious capital campaign in the museum's history, had these major objectives: greatly increased endowment, additional earned income, renovation and modernization of the entire museum, and a new wing to double the gallery space.

The state and city played key roles in making the program possible. The state legislature created a Trust for Cultural Resources of the City of New York, a public benefit corporation which could act for the museum in this venture. The city, recognizing the financial and cultural benefits it would derive from the program, waived the condominium owners' tax payments for the museum's use.

The Trust provided most of the financing (through bond issues totaling $60 million) to renovate and modernize the museum and add a new six-story wing. It also arranged for the sale of the Modern's air rights to a developer for the construction of a commercially financed 44-story condominium tower above the new wing.

From this complex program, the museum has gained—and will continue to gain—important benefits. Its building has been completely modernized and greatly enlarged. It will receive additional annual income of $3 million from the condominium owners' tax equivalency payments, which will be paid to the museum through the Trust when the bond debt and other Trust obligations are met.

The museum, with $17 million from the sale of its air rights and $58 million in campaign contributions, ultimately will realize a total of $75 million in additional endowment. In addition, the museum will gain greater annual income from increased memberships which the enlarged building will accommodate, and greater earned income from increased admissions and sales of auxiliary services.

If these impressive benefits seem just to have fallen into place, if the complex and innovative program that produced them appears to have emerged full-blown from the outset, nothing could be farther from the truth. The program evolved in stages, each marked by its own set of obstacles. Only by overcoming the obstacles of each stage could the next be undertaken.

Persevering volunteer leadership was essential to the program's success. Such leadership was provided in full measure—and during a period more than double the duration of the traditional three-year capital campaign—by campaign chairperson Mrs. John D. Rockefeller 3rd, the museum's president; William S. Paley, the museum's board chairman; and David Rockefeller, the museum's immediate past board chairman.

From the very initiation of the development program, Mrs. Rockefeller was steadfast in her belief in its viability. Infinitely patient and kindly, she was unrelentingly firm in sustaining the program during its growing pains. Its success is due in no small measure to the first-class attention she devoted to its advancement and to her continuing efforts in soliciting financial support.

With characteristic effectiveness, Mr. Paley brought his highly developed critical faculties to bear on the program as it evolved; he then gave it his full endorsement and support. Importantly, he helped set the example for other major supporters by the generosity of his own financial commitment—a commitment which he significantly increased on a number of occasions during the campaign.

Unwavering in his advocacy, David Rockefeller exerted his considerable influence by taking a leadership position at critical times in the evolution of the develoment program. Generous in his own financial commitments to the program, he timed his infusions of support so that they would serve most effectively to stimulate and inspire others to increase their pledges to the campaign.

After the program as initially conceived was launched, Donald B. Marron, chairman of Paine Webber Inc. and a museum trustee, contributed importantly as chairman of the expansion committee responsible for development and financing of the museum's expansion and renovation. Appropriately, he also served as a trustee of the Trust for Cultural Resources of the City of New York.

The advancement of a development program usually requires an effective partnership of volunteer leadership and professional staff; the success of the Modern's program reflected creditably on the participation and assistance of Richard E. Oldenburg, museum director, and John Limpert, Jr., director of development.

For most of my fund-raising career, I considered it absolutely essential that an institution undertake a feasibility study before it embarked upon a capital campaign. I was sufficiently rigid about this position to turn down prospective clients who said they didn't need a study or couldn't take the time for one because they had to initiate solicitation of pledges immediately.

I still believe that there are very important reasons for a pre-campaign study. It can indicate the feasibility of the goal and, if an institution's objectives are completely unattainable, can save the institution from embarking upon a costly campaign doomed to failure.

Even when an institution says it is going to launch a campaign, regardless of the feasibility of its goal, it would benefit greatly

81

from a study to determine how best to implement its campaign objectives.

The study would indicate the extent of the funds it could raise; the period of time needed to achieve the goal; the type of campaign that would be most effective; the sources of support and what each could give; the strength of the case for the campaign; the availability of leaders, workers, and prospective donors; the presence of conditions that could affect the campaign adversely; the requirement for cultivation of prospects; the extent of the need for professional fund-raising assistance; and a budget adequate for the campaign.

These important advantages for a capital campaign are difficult to dismiss, but institutions have done it. Indeed, some of these institutions have launched campaigns for very ambitious capital objectives—and have been successful. Two factors may account for their success: their past campaign experience may have provided them with substantial guidance, or their development departments may have produced the equivalent of a study's findings.

In recent years, I have become somewhat less rigid in insisting upon a feasibility study before I would agree to counsel a campaign. In the few instances where I have agreed, I assured myself through preliminary discussion that (all factors considered) the campaign had a decent chance to succeed, that the institution's urgent needs required such a campaign, and that the campaign leadership clearly understood that in no way was I to be held responsible for the feasibility of the goal.

With this protection (somewhat less than air-tight), I felt that I could counsel in good conscience a worthwhile institution seeking to raise the capital funds it needed to advance its essential objectives.

Lew Bowen served as a senior vice president of the Brakeley, John Price Jones firm for a relatively short time. He subsequently set himself up as Lewis H. Bowen Associates in White Plains, New York, and functioned as an individual consultant.

He was in New York City rarely and I therefore saw him infrequently. At the last few luncheons of the Friday Club That Meets on Monday, of which he was the moving force, he struck me as having changed radically. I recall trying not to recognize the change that had come over him.

He could have had Alzheimer's Disease, as his wife described it. She informed me that he had been hospitalized and, later, that he had died. It was my lot to write his obituary. In assembling his biographical data, I was impressed anew with the breadth of his professional experience which extended to three fields—financial reporting, publicity, and fund raising.

After graduating from Haverford College, Bowen was a financial reporter for the *New York Journal of Commerce, The New York Herald Tribune,* and *U.S. News* (later *U.S. News and World Report.*) During World War II, he served as national publicity director for the American Red Cross and he later became associate editor of the Gallup Poll.

He began his fund-raising career with the John Price Jones Company. Later, he became a vice-president of Kersting, Brown & Company, where he worked for 10 years, leaving in 1959 to join me in forming Bowen & Gurin, Inc.

Bowen was a former president of the National Public Relations Council of Health and Welfare Services and of the Saw Mill Audubon Society. He was a member of the board of the Columbia University School of Social Work.

Thus, Lewis H. Bowen, 1911-1977.

I would have liked to include other things about him that those who knew him would recognize, things that were just as important as the professional positions he filled. I would have liked to note his warmheartedness and openness to people, his broad human sympathies, his lack of prejudice and bigotry. I didn't mention these things because, as a former newspaperman, I knew they would be excised from my text by the press.

Death can make hypocrites of us. But I can, with complete honesty, say that while Bowen and I had problems in working together and differences over the management of the firm we formed, we never lost respect for each other or confidence in each other's integrity. We had disagreements, but we also had mutual trust.

Kathrine M. Ockenden, who managed the $10 million Ford Foundation matching campaign at WNET/Channel 13 while I served as consultant, moved to the New York Philharmonic in 1977 as development director. I heard from her soon after she assumed that position because the orchestra needed a feasibility study to learn whether it could raise $18 million in additional endowment by 1982.

Remembering the difficulty the Philharmonic experienced in raising endowment funds in the mid-1960s, I requested—and Amyas Ames, the board chairman, agreed—that the study could test whether it was possible to raise either $18 million in additional endowment or $1.1 million in additional annual income (the equivalent of what $18 million in endowment could generate annually).

Through the study, I learned that only $12 million in endowment was a realistic expectation in a three-year campaign. I therefore recommended a continuing financial development program and, at the outset, a three-year campaign for at least $12 million in additional endowment or its equivalent in annual operating funds.

This approach was initially approved and I was engaged to counsel the campaign. Later, however, it was decided that instead of seeking $12 million over three years, the campaign would undertake to raise all of the $18 million needed in additional endowment regardless of how long it would take.

I had known Mr. Ames from the previous endowment campaign when he had served as president of the Philharmonic. Since then, he had retired from Kidder, Peabody & Co., Inc. and become a full-time volunteer serving as board chairman of both Lincoln Center for the Performing Arts and the New York Philharmonic.

He was the most effective chairman available for the endowment campaign and he agreed to serve as its co-chairman with

Sampson R. Field, president of the Philharmonic. At the same time, and with his other hat, Mr. Ames started a $20 million endowment campaign for Lincoln Center, and provided the volunteer leaderhsip for that fund-raising effort as well.

Thus, he was heading two campaigns—one for an umbrella organization and the other for a constituent institution. I was afraid that, even if these two compaigns were not conflicting, they were competing at least to some extent for his attention. My fear was self-centered: since my interest was solely in the Philharmonic campaign, I wanted his full attention focused on it.

There was a concern in January of 1981 when the pledges to the campaign, which totaled $12.1 million, seemed to plateau; but then I realized that it was just about three years since the campaign had been launched. Our feasibility study finding that $12 million could be raised in three years had proven to be on target.

In December 1982, however, the full goal was achieved—thanks to a bequest by Mrs. Charles A. Dana, who had been a director of the Philharmonic until her death and who had earlier contributed substantially to the campaign through the Charles A. Dana Foundation she had headed. Her contributions therefore amounted to more than $5 million of the $18 million goal!

The Philharmonic had attained its campaign objective in just about five years. In addition, annual giving to the orchestra, which our study showed had the potential for considerable growth, rose sharply during the period of the endowment campaign, an experience which is highly unusual.

Since Lincoln Center's $20 million endowment campaign goal was attained a year earlier, Mr. Ames achieved the distinction of having successfully led endowment campaigns for two related organizations simultaneously.

I confess that I have never been receptive to computers and have actually been resistant to them. Schooled in the humanities, I have been largely ignorant of science and, worse still, uninterested in being informed. To me, using a computer is taking a mechanistic approach to fund raising.

I have never forgotten the early experience of colleges with computers. When they were introduced in the 1960s, as I recall, a development office was in chaos: the computers didn't work and the previous systems had been dismantled for the computerization process. It used to take from one to two years before the kinks were worked out and the computer functioned properly.

I must now assume that computers are here to stay, and that they are invaluable and probably will become indispensable, but I am relieved that I am not starting anew in fund raising and would have to be schooled in their use.

Early in 1982, the American Association of Fund-Raising Counsel established a Technology Committee, chaired by Arthur D. Raybin, who heads a member firm. That fall, he sent a questionnaire to all AAFRC members, which sought information for the committee's guidance.

The lead question asked if my firm was using any of the following technology and, if so, what brand and model: microprocessor-based equipment, computers (mainframes, mini or micro), word processors, facsimile transmission, programmable calculators, mobile telephones, video, data transmission, and telecommunications.

Luckily for me, the questionnaire listed "other" and I answered: Typewriter, Underwood, 1934.

To the follow-up question—how is my firm using "this technology?"—I replied: By hand (two fingers).

And to the last question I could answer—what role should the Association play concerning technology?—I wrote: For those fund raisers whom Ed Gemmell calls "mechanics," technology should be promoted up to their eyeballs.

Fortunately for fund raising, I am one of the last of a disappearing breed.

Fund raisers who are paid are called professional fund raisers, which distinguishes them from volunteer fund raisers who are not paid. But is fund raising, as practiced by paid fund raisers, a profession? This complicated question, insofar as I know, has never been answered satisfactorily in the affirmative.

I assume that fund raising, to qualify technically as a profession, would have to comprise a body of recognized knowledge and experience, and be a discipline taught at institutions of higher learning; and its practitioners would have to be licensed by the state, pledged to observe a code of ethics, and subject to being held accountable by an appropriately constituted agency of authority in the field.

In recent years, fund raising has made important advances toward achieving professional status. A considerable body of knowledge and experience has been accumulated: a total of more than 100 books on the subject have been published.

Colleges are now including courses on fund raising, which are being taught by practitioners in the field. But these courses are elective and fund raisers are not required to take them. In addition, men and women without any training or experience occasionally are offered positions in fund raising by reputable organizations.

Fund raisers are not licensed, though some states currently require them to be registered. Practitioners, for the most part, are the product of on-the-job training. There are no standards of competence that fund raisers must meet.

The National Society of Fund Raising Executives has initiated a certification program in which practitioners can elect to participate. Many—but certainly not all—fund raisers have already taken part in the program.

The American Association of Fund-Raising Counsel, which has long had a Fair Practice Code (Appendix G) to which its members subscribe, has the mechanism to censure or expel a member firm that violates the Code's provisions. It cannot, of course, exercise any authority over non-member firms.

The National Society of Fund Raising Executives, which in recent years has formulated a Code of Ethics and Professional Practices for its members' observance, lacks the mechanism to enforce a member's compliance with the Code's provisions.

Judging by the technical requirements which I assume are germane, fund raising is not yet a profession. It is a trade, business, and occupation, if one views it in a commercial sense; an art, if one sees it in esthetic terms; and a calling, if one brings to it a religious zeal.

Perhaps for any vocation, however rigidly it qualifies as a profession, professionalism ultimately must be viewed as a goal, rather than a resting place. Certainly for fund raising that goal is being advanced impressively by the American Association of Fund-Raising Counsel under the long-time direction of its president, John J. Schwartz, and by the National Society of Fund Raising Executives under its current president, J. Richard Wilson.

It has annoyed me that some fund-raising counseling firms which could qualify for membership in the American Association of Fund-Raising Counsel have chosen to remain on the outside—to benefit from, but not contribute to, the Association's program.

Being an old curmudgeon, I took it upon myself several years ago to write to several qualified firms which were not members of the Association and which, in my view, were enjoying a free ride. They had elaborate excuses but no interest in coming aboard and helping to pay the freight.

I wish I could say that member firms have never questioned the Association's financial value for them; a few have. On one such occasion, in the late 1970s, David S. Ketchum, board chairman of Ketchum, Inc., responded with characteristic statesmanship to this question.

He noted that over the years his firm had invested more than three-quarters of a million dollars in dues and expenses, and in direct return never received one dollar in fees. He said it was the belief of his company, however, that it had received its money's worth.

Why? Because of the national recognition and reputation the Association enjoys. Because its publications are authoritative and are quoted at the highest level of government. Because if the Association did not exist, it would have to be reinvented for the mutual protection of its members and the collective visibility it provides. Because, with American philanthropy being challenged today as never before at both national and state levels, it would be impossible for his firm, or any other, to make a significant impact on these challenges without the Association.

This reasoned affirmation of the Association's value came from a second-generation fund raiser whose firm was a charter member of the Association and who served as its board chairman, as did his father, Carlton G. Ketchum, before him.

From the beginning of my counseling career, I was less afraid of telling clients the unpleasant truth than I was of concealing it from them. And over the years I have come to regard myself as expendable—in the sense that I cannot temper my advice to clients for the purpose of retaining their approval. If they don't want straightforward advice, they don't want me—and vice versa.

Younger consultants have told me that I can get away with this attitude and that I can afford to maintain it because it's easier to be brave when one is an antique and no longer needs the business. What they have difficulty in understanding is that it is more dangerous not to level with clients.

Fund raising can be a troublesome responsibility for volunteer leaders of gift-supported organizations. The most effective fund-raising methods are not the easiest for them. If they are occasionally resistant, it is because they are only human. But they also want to succeed.

A consultant who advises them candidly may not be telling them what they would prefer to hear, but he is doing his best to protect them. He is helping them meet their responsibilities to their organizations; he is helping them to succeed.

A consultant should never underestimate volunteer leaders. Even those with decidedly set opinions usually respect a consultant who disagrees with them—if he knows what he's talking about.

At a meeting some years ago with the volunteer leaders of a major institution, I thought it my duty to broach what I knew would be an unpopular suggestion. I felt sure they would react adversely—and they did.

After the meeting, however, the president of the institution took me aside and said, "Don't let us discourage you. Keep telling us what we should hear."

I relate this incident to strengthen the faint-hearted in our business.

I guess what I am saying ultimately is that a relationship—in business as well as in our personal lives—is without value if it is not honest and open. Through much of our lives, most of us try to disguise ourselves; we don a veneer which we assume is more acceptable.

As I've grown older, I find I'm being more and more myself (not necessarily an unmixed blessing, as my friends have noted) and less and less reliant on disguises, which don't work anyway. One's self comes through, regardless. That is all one has, and as flawed as one may be, it's a lot better than a misrepresented version that clinks as falsely as a lead nickel.

It was my impression that A. Chauncey Newlin was most responsible for getting the Metropolitan Opera interested in undertaking a capital campaign in 1973, though he was not the only member of the opera's board to recognize the need for additional endowment and expendable funds.

Representing the Henry L. and Grace Doherty Charitable Foundation, Mr. Newlin conveyed to the opera board of directors an offer of a matching challenge: the foundation would provide $3 million if the Metropolitan raised $9 million by the end of 1974.

But the foundation, with Mr. Newlin's guidance, also recognized the opera's greater financial needs. It therefore suggested that the Metropolitan undertake to raise an additional $60 million to ensure its financial stability in the foreseeable future.

The Gurin Group was retained in December of 1973 to conduct a study to determine the opera's potential ability to raise capital funds. We recommended that a number of preliminary requirements be met before the opera embarked on a long-range capital development program, of which the Doherty Foundation matching challenge would be the first phase.

This study enabled me to work closely with the president of the Metropolitan, George S. Moore, former chairman of Citicorp. Production costs had risen appreciably; and Mr. Moore believed that, in addition to raising much more endowment, the opera had to reduce expenses (mainly in the lavishness of its productions).

Soon after he approved the study recommendations and gained the board's acceptance, he resigned and went into what he termed retirement. It included, as I recall him saying, only looking after some investment interest in Texas, Venezuela, and Spain (where he then intended to reside with his family).

The new leadership under William Rockefeller, who succeeded Mr. Moore, called me in several times to ask if I thought the Metropolitan was ready to launch a capital fund effort. Each time, after learning that the preliminary requirements I had specified in the study report had not been met, I had no choice but to answer in the negative.

And then I was no longer called. Another consultant, Wayne Horvath, had been brought in from Boston. He served for several years, I believe, but a capital campaign was not undertaken during that time, either.

Only after Frank E. Taplin was elected president of the Metropolitan—and Arthur Raybin, as the consultant, provided an updated feasibility study—was a campaign launched. The goal was an impressive $100 million. Mr. Taplin knew fund raising and worked at it. I'd no doubt that the goal would be achieved.

I must confess that if there is one thing my mind apparently does not care to retain, it's the various ways of making planned (deferred) gifts. I can rehearse them for use on a particular occasion, but then I promptly forget them.

For many years, I noted how the average institution would appoint a planned giving specialist to its staff and how he would address inquiries to prospects other than those who should be the first to participate in such a program—the members of the board. I also observed how the average board would appoint a planned giving committee and then send it out on its own to see what it could attract from others.

Obviously, the effective way to launch such a program would be to have the board members pledge their active participation. With the board setting the example, others could best be influenced to make planned gifts. But I never knew a board to take this action.

I therefore concluded in the mid-1970s that the most practical—and certainly the most painless—method of introducing a planned giving program to an institution was to integrate it into a capital campaign (assuming, of course, that institution is engaged in such a campaign).

A planned gift could be suggested as an add-on to what a donor pledges in cash, securities, and other property—particularly when he pledges inadequately or would like to give more. It also could be suggested to a prospect who cannot give from current financial resources.

And during a capital campaign's second-round solicitation, board members and other major donors could be interested in planned gift add-ons when, without them, they would be unable to make significant commitments.

An institution can best encourage donors to make planned gift add-ons by establishing the policy that campaign recognition would be accorded them for the total of their gifts, including planned gifts. The institution would stand to lose little—and could gain much—by such a policy, since it would not otherwise receive the planned gifts.

At the conclusion of a capital campaign, then, the institution would have obtained planned gifts from some of its most important donors, including board members. And with these gifts, it would have embarked successfully upon a planned giving program.

My mind can play with concepts like this, but heaven help me if I'm asked without warning to list the various ways of making planned gifts and recite their individual advantages.

\*    \*    \*

Fund-raising consultants can—and many do—work well past the usual retirement age. In other fields of endeavor, gray or balding heads are currently out of fashion, but they are acceptable and sometimes even an advantage in fund raising where they apparently convey the impression of maturity and experience, which add up to judgment—the main desideratum.

Why do so many fund-raising consultants (myself included) want to work past the customary retirement age? I cannot speak authoritatively for others, but my hunch is that they want to hang in there not just because they are accepted or because they want to continue to lead active lives.

There is something about fund raising that never loses its hold on fund raisers. I think that's because it gives them a sense of satisfaction, of accomplishment in a worthwhile cause. I experience that satisfaction today when I pass a museum or school that was built through a campaign I counseled, or when I read about a program or service that I had some hand in making possible.

And for that satisfaction, I feel some obligation to the practice of fund raising, which I try to meet by supporting the American Association of Fund-Raising Counsel and the National Society of Fund Raising Executives, as well as by sharing with younger fund raisers whatever I've been able to learn over the years.

# 4

# Playing the Elder Statesman

It is certainly true in fund raising, as it is in other fields, that when one is up in years and has worked long in the business, he is sorely tempted to appear as an elder statesman. I confess that I have found this temptation too strong to resist.

And so I explored many a path to elder statesmanship that is open to an aging fund raiser with the competence and commitment to stay the course. If my experiences are at all typical, there is practically no limit to the extent to which an older fund raiser can go to satisfy a still vigorous ego.

An almost certain path, though by no means free of risk, is to make a forecast of future trends in fund raising and/or philanthropy. I have presumed to make such forecasts and have survived them—mainly because they were adequately hedged, and, where they weren't, because few if any readers check back to see where I have missed the mark.

In 1979, I presented a forecast, "Fund Raising in the Future," before the Greater New York Chapter of the National Society of Fund Raising Executives. And in 1980 I exploited the forecast further by adapting it for inclusion as a chapter on "Likely Future Trends" in my book, *What Volunteers Should Know for Successful Fund Raising*.

Since the book was written in 1980 (though published in 1981) before the advent of the Reagan Administration, at least a few of my forecasts were wide of the mark. Fortunately I was rescued: my publisher asked me to update the text for a second edition in 1982—in light of the Reagan Administration cutbacks in federal support of social welfare, health, education, and arts programs, and the effects of the Economic Recovery Tax Act of 1981 on charitable giving.

The seeker of an elder statesman image need not always take the initiative in offering to forecast trends; sometimes he is asked for his predictions. Members of the press assume that, because a fund raiser is supposed to know how fund raising functioned in the past and how it is currently practiced, he is competent to project future developments.

Queried by the press, a fund raiser is usually on fairly safe ground: his comments are either edited out of the story that appears or they are sufficiently mangled to enable him to claim that they in no way reflected what he said.

The same degree of protection is afforded the fund raiser who appears on television and radio talk shows. I've appeared on both and felt I was in no danger because of two built-in protections—a talk show participant usually has no time to make a substantive statement, and no one who counts ever watches at the odd times such shows are aired.

The overly cautious type of aging fund raiser can take refuge in hedging every tame comment he makes with such precautionary conditions as "other factors being equal" or "if present influences continue." Of course, he will never be asked to appear again, but at least he'll escape whole.

Forecasts can start to pale even for the elder statesman who has been addicted to them. I tried to shake the habit late in 1982 by writing "Some Fund-Raising Changes: A Backward Glance" (Appendix H), a critical review covering the past few decades, for *Fund Raising Review,* which is published by the American Association of Fund-Raising Counsel. Such an exercise feeds the ego because it implies that the author was practicing fund raising in those decades at a level that enabled him to influence those changes.

\*    \*    \*

A close relative of forecasting is the recording of trends. In mid-1969, I delivered a paper on "Recent Fund-Raising Developments in America" at a conference of professional fund raisers that was held at The Grove, in Harpenden, Hertfordshire, the headquarters of Hooker, Craigmyle & Company, Ltd., the English fund-raising counseling firm.

I gained additional mileage from this talk the following February when *Alma Mater*, the journal of the American Alumni Council, adapted it for an article titled, "Thirty Trends in the 'New Fund Raising'" (Appendix I). And, indicative of long-range benefits of trend-spotting, most of the trends I noted in 1969 were cited as still pertinent in 1982 by John P. Butler II, president of Barnes & Roche, Inc., in an article that year in *NSFRE Journal*, which is published by the National Society of Fund Raising Executives.

Writing articles for professional fund-raising journals is standard practice for an elder statesman. His name, if not his message, is noted by other fund raisers, some of whom are too busy raising funds to take the time to write articles, and most of whom cannot write even though fund raising is the art of persuasion.

This path to eminence as an elder statesman is paved by the paucity of even mediocre material available to professional fund-raising journals, which traditionally and probably necessarily do not pay for articles. An elder statesman who can write and seeks only to be published is a valued resource for such publications.

Now if an aging fund raiser has a book published, he becomes almost automatically an elder statesman. And if he knows how—and takes the time—to promote the book, he has a property (as they say in Hollywood) which has a practically endless potential for exploitation—the book's and his own professional status.

If he does not undertake the book's promotion, he might as well forget about it, for a publisher seldom really believes in promoting his books. He usually puts out a number of books in the marketplace (adding to the 50,000-odd new books published annually in this country), and then watches to see whether one catches fire on its own. Only when a book succeeds on its own—when it doesn't need any help—does the publisher decide to invest in its promotion.

If the author decides to promote his book, he should start with the safe assumption that his royalties will be negligible. Therefore, he may as well order a good quantity at the author's discount and distribute complimentary copies to clients, prospective clients, leaders of fund-raising associations, editors of professional fund-raising journals, and reviewers to whom the publisher failed to send review copies.

I recall in the 1960s David Ogilvy telling me that his *Confessions of an Advertising Man* was largely responsible for many of his major clients. In a much smaller way, I received inquiries from prospective clients that were attributable to *What Volunteers Should Know for Successful Fund Raising*. But in one way, I went Ogilvy one better: I told prospective clients I was not in a position to accept any more business. But then I felt obliged to recommend other firms which I thought would be appropriate for them. That service, of course, helps to cement the status of an elder statesman.

By undertaking to promote his book, the author will not necessarily increase his royalties. It is one thing to gain publicity for the book; it is quite another thing to have it purchased. A prospective buyer first would have to locate it in a bookstore, and I have never found two stores that stack books on fund raising under the same subject—a reflection, I believe, of a general difficulty to categorize fund raising. It once took me 20 minutes to find my own book in a chain bookstore and the chain had ordered 1,000 of them.

But the author should understand that he's really not after increased royalties; he's promoting his book to establish or advance his elder statesmanship. He can gain the kind of ego satisfaction I confess that I felt when I learned that the Children's Aid Society in New York ordered 50 copies for its volunteer leaders; that the National YWCA ordered 100 copies for its affiliate leaders; and that Ketchum, Inc., the largest fund-raising counseling firm in the country, provided copies to its clients and new staff members.

\*    \*    \*

An elder statesman is always setting things straight for the record. If any opinion of doubtful value or validity is advanced at a meeting, he is quick to take the floor and make clear its questionable merit. If an article is written that reflects unfairly on professional fund raising or philanthropy, he leaps to his typewriter to register a reasoned dissent.

A case in point occurred when the October 1982 issue of *NSFRE Newsletter* of the Greater New York Chapter, National Society of Fund Raising Executives, printed a letter to the editor from Anne New, a long-time member of the chapter, in which she asked whether it was not time to reexamine the Society's stand against fund raisers charging on a commission or percentage basis.

Concerned by the reasons her letter cited, I flung my cloak of elder statesmanship about me and whipped off a letter to the editor answering the question she raised. My measured response (Appendix J), which appeared in the next issue of *NSFRE Newsletter*, was necessitated by the sensitive nature of the question for fund raisers.

News items offer occasional opportunities for an elder statesman to take to task the press or the people it quotes. Such an opportunity occurred on December 4, 1982, when *The New York Times*, in a page one story, practically invited a letter to the editor. The letter I could have written, if counseling duties had not completely absorbed me at the time, is included as Appendix K.

An elder statesman stands by the old verities in fund raising—such as strengthening the case and the board, training volunteers to be effective solicitors, and urging them to solicit in person their prospects capable of substantial gifts.

Protectively, he moves quickly to counter any perceived threat to established fund-raising practice and terminology. A case in point: the relatively recent introduction of advertising jargon—specifically "marketing" and "market research"—seems to me to represent no more than different and less desirable terms for traditional fund-raising techniques. I made this observation in an article I wrote for the April 1984 issue of *Fund Raising Management* magazine, in which I employed a narrative form to heighten interest (it is included as Appendix L).

An elder statesman does not rush to embrace new techniques and technologies until they have been tested adequately and shown to be effective. His posture here coincides with the policy of the old *Saturday Evening Post*, which proudly proclaimed that when something appeared in the *Post* it was established. The magazine never wanted the sometimes dubious distinction of being first.

This attitude does not have to be overly conservative or anti-progressive. The elder statesman takes due notice of all that is new and promising, but he has learned to maintain a critical reserve and withhold his endorsement until the results are in.

Not surprisingly, however, he is continually alert and receptive to new opportunities for needed services by the causes he serves, recognizing that philanthropy must keep abreast of the changing needs of our society.

In this respect, he feels a spiritual kinship with John D. Rockefeller 3rd, an elder statesman in philanthropy, who in 1964 observed that "it is essential that we display a greater readiness to venture, to take risks, to dare. . . We are prone to be too complacent, too willing to conform, too ready to settle for the tried and proven. Rather than venture, we tend to hang back, neglectful of the new needs of today and the impatient future."

Even in fund raising, however, an elder statesman doesn't always play it safe; he recognizes when calculated risks are indicated. An example could be his willingness to appear on a television or radio program which is planned to discuss "charitable frauds" and "fund-raising abuses."

He can justify his participation—and defend himself from criticism—by taking the position that he would otherwise have lost an opportunity to correct unfounded charges and to present a balanced view of such charges which have some basis in fact.

I made such an appearance—in tandem with E. Burr Gibson, who heads the Marts & Lundy fund-raising counseling firm—on WOR-TV Channel 9 (New York City) in late 1982; and compounded the benefits of our participation with an article (included as Appendix M), which I wrote for *Fund Raising Review* in early 1983.

An elder statesman enhances his stature when he shows that he is not a blind follower of accepted practice but a continual challenger of standard procedure, when he provides evidence that he is at the cutting edge of professional thinking and exploration.

Evidence I've offered includes an article I wrote for the October 1983 issue of *Fund Raising Management* (Appendix N), in which I questioned long-held assumptions in the strategy of raising capital funds and coined the term *fund raising by objective.*

Related evidence were the positions I took in *What Volunteers Should Know for Successful Fund Raising.* In that book, I ruled out as no longer applicable the "rule of thirds" that had been used for decades in structuring gift tables for capital campaigns, and proposed in its place a "specific situation formula" that places greater emphasis on the giving potential of the individual organization's actual prospects than on a general rule.

I also used the medium of the book to discourage the continued use of an evaluations committee for rating the giving potential of capital campaign prospects, noting that appropriately selected members of soliciting committees are better able to make such judgments.

And I developed 19 differences between annual and capital campaigns—a number far greater than the three or four differences that were usually cited.

Such evidence, incidentally, helped assure professional fund raisers that the book's value was not limited to volunteers.

*     *     *

An elder statesman cannot be infallible—nor should he try to be. I recall the late Sy Seymour, certainly an elder statesman of the first rank, once saying that a fund raiser can't afford to be right more than 85 percent of the time. Beyond that, I'm sure, he'd be unbearable, unfit for association with his fellow man.

Many years ago, I was asked to critique a board meeting of the newly formed National Foundation for Ileitis and Colitis. At the meeting, discussions were turbulent, issues were hotly debated, tempers were short, and emotions were rampant.

Later, when I was asked for my critique, I said: "I am impressed with the strength of your commitment, the extent of your service to the organization. Your differing views are honestly held. But can't you express them without tearing each other apart?"

Irwin Rosenthal, the Foundation's president, smiled tolerantly. "You don't understand," he told me; "that's the way we make love."


An aging fund raiser can evidence his elder statesmanship by taking every appropriate occasion to simplify fund-raising language. An authority in a given discipline is usually one who is so clear on his subject that he does not have to take refuge behind the patois or technical jargon that lesser practitioners find so comforting for their psyches.

He can speak simply and clearly—but at the same time he must make certain it is generally understood that his special status permits him to speak in that way. Thus, his simple speech is, in effect, a criticism of the abstruseness and pretension of lesser practitioners.

He can employ this same technique in discussing and analyzing seemingly complex fund-raising problems. After he has focused in on the heart of the problem, laid it bare, and indicated its solution, he can also indicate—however obliquely—what he thinks of those who in their ignorance saw complexity.

\*    \*    \*

A sure sign of an elder statesman is a fund raiser who is so confident of his credentials that he can answer a difficult question by saying, "I don't know." Obviously, such a shocking response cannot be attempted by anyone of lesser stature.

But even an elder statesman should immediately assist his audience in recognizing the wisdom of his response by citing the story about Albert D. Lasker, the former Chicago advertising genius and super salesman who was one of the first philanthropists to take a day off from business and devote it to raising funds for a favorite charity.

According to the story (as I recall it from John Gunther's *Taken at the Flood*), Lasker and Phillip D. Block, a close friend who headed the Inland Steel Company, made a solicitation call on a prosperous banker. Lasker pressed the banker, who had already made a contribution, to add to it, but the banker adamantly refused.

Lasker then said to the banker, "Of course, you certainly do not owe it to us to give just because we call on you; but after all, we are busy men, and if it is important enough for us to take a day off from our business just to see you, surely you have the duty to give us a reason for your refusal."

"The reason is that I don't like mince pie," the banker said.

"What kind of reason is that?" Lasker asked.

"If you don't want to do a thing," the banker said, "one reason is as good as any other."

The elder statesman should then make the point that there are some problems in fund raising, as there are in other fields, for which there are no ready answers. Obviously, he is smart enough to recognize such problems.


An elder statesman may occasionally view with alarm, but mostly he takes the long view that, despite present adversity, conditions ultimately will improve and perhaps be even better than before. He keeps his head and his balance, remembering previous occasions which seemed utterly beyond hope.

When the passage of the Economic Recovery Tax Act of 1981 deprived donors of some of the tax benefits they had enjoyed previously, there was considerable gloom at the outset among some fund raisers. To help correct this attitude (which in itself could adversely affect philanthropic giving), the Greater New York Chapter, National Society of Fund Raising Executives, scheduled a seminar of leaders in the profession to assess the likely effects of the new tax law.

Almost without exception, the speakers took a positive view. The text of my remarks was the passage in St. Paul's first Letter to the Corinthians which begins, "Though I speak with the tongues of men and of angels, and have not charity. . ." and ends with, "And now abideth faith, hope, charity, these three; but the greatest of these is charity."

I said that "in this time of concern for philanthropy, I had repaired for guidance to I Corinthians. I read and reread very carefully this long and insightful passage, and I couldn't find the slightest mention of tax benefits for the donors of charitable contributions."

An older fund raiser grows in stature when he turns down, because of principle, an inquiry from a prestigious institution. In the 1960s, I was asked to counsel a school at Harvard; fortunately, it was not difficult to decline, as the school would not agree to a pre-campaign feasibility study.

Actually, therefore, I turned down the offer in self-defense: I didn't want to be associated with a campaign when I hadn't had the opportunity to test its feasibility. But that didn't make any difference. The point was that I had turned down a Harvard school, and that became known in professional fund-raising circles. There is no telling how far that declination, if properly exploited, could have carried me.

\*    \*    \*

A widely recognized way of donning the mantle of an elder statesman is to be available to counsel younger and less experienced fund raisers. But an older practitioner must be careful that this avocation doesn't become his vocation.

In the 1960s, I declined a second term as president of the Greater New York Chapter, National Society of Fund Raisers (as the organization was then known), because too many of its members called on me for career advice during working hours.

Over the past decade, a considerable number of fund raisers sought my advice about setting up their own firms. Most of them were not ready, in my judgment, and I told them so. Some of them were not sufficiently experienced; they would have been in the awkward position of seeking to counsel staff fund raisers with knowledge and skills superior to their own. Others did not have the entrepreneurial instinct to succeed on their own.

The timid ones would eliminate themselves after my first question, "Would you get nervous when Friday comes and there is no paycheck?" And if that question didn't do the trick, I'd ask, "How long are you prepared to carry yourself financially until you can sign up clients?"

Almost all of them would agree with my advice that it was best to line up one or two clients—if that would be possible while they were still working for an organization—before embarking on their own. The ones who succeeded, as I recall, were those who did precisely that.

In the last few years, as fund raisers interested in becoming consultants continued to seek my advice, I compiled a checklist of questions they could ask themselves to judge their readiness for such a career change. I include it as Appendix O.


An elder statesman occasionally is called upon by institutions (some of which he has never served) to advise them as a "friend at court" on how to find fund raisers for their staffs and how to judge their competence. He therefore usually keeps two lists for this free service: one, of institutions with position vacancies; and the other, of fund raisers looking for positions.

It is rewarding experience to help match the right fund raiser with the right position, and it provides a needed service for philanthropic organizations, as well as for the fund-raising field. A few of us aged practitioners give more time to this service than we can sometimes afford, despite its satisfying rewards.

A variation of such service is when an elder statesman—again on a free-of-charge basis—is asked to assist an institution with a problem it is experiencing with its development staff. Sometimes I found that I could serve quite openly in such a situation, with the presence and prticipation of staff. Other times I could see that I had to work clandestinely in order to serve effectively, as the knowledge of my involvement could prove embarrassing to the staff. When the problem involved another fund-raising counseling firm, the situation was more sticky but my approach was the same.


An elder statesman would think it gauche and unprofessional to claim any credit for the success of a campaign he counseled. He would give credit to the volunteer fund raisers, and make light of his own role.

I have groaned inwardly when I occasionally have heard a fund-raising consultant or development director say that he has raised the funds to meet an organization's campaign goal. Volunteers should—and are in the best position to—ask for campaign commitments; professional fund raisers are properly functioning when they advise and assist volunteers in becoming effective solicitors.

This distinction has been drawn so clearly so often over so many years that it is difficult to understand how some so-called professionals in the business have not heard of it or, knowing it, evidence no inclination to observe it.

It is probably an increasing sensitivity to this breach of professionalism that underlies my own tendency in recent years to make light of whatever part I may have played in helping to insure a campaign's success. I usually say that the volunteer fund raisers succeeded despite my advice.

A good professional should not need credit; he does his job well, which should be satisfaction enough. And by not seeking credit, he often is accorded more than he deserves.

Eccentricity—short of senility, of course—can further the image of elder statesmanship: the absentminded professor act which implies that mental activity is going on at a high level. This act is safe for those elder statesmen whose words do not give them away or who have the native cunning to keep whatever advice they may have to themselves.

It is a distinct asset for an elder statesman to look the part. It helps if his hair has silvered or even disappeared altogether. I remember being told by Dr. Abram Leon Sacher in 1940, just before I attended a meeting with Albert Einstein at Princeton, not to feel like I was in the presence of infinity. But that caution was for naught when I faced that wispy halo of silvery hair floating above an ageless countenance.

For the older fund raiser who secretly longs for elder statesmanship but feels self-conscious or overly sensitive about taking any steps to attain it, I can only say that playing the elder statesman is no more esthetically degrading than playing the doting grandfather or any other role available to—and suitable for—a senior member of our society.

It's bad enough to be aged (my father used to say, "it's no fun being old"); but to be an elder and not a statesman—that would be (as my godson would say) "the living end."

# Not for Princeton Alone

*It is now conceivable, technologically, to annihilate a continent or to rid mankind of disease. How we respond to this challenge (and to others of equal urgency) will determine how we live—and whether we live.*

America has known challenges before—crises which have also threatened its well-being and survival. Perhaps never before, however, has the nation faced so many complex and urgent problems simultaneously.

Significantly, too, the major problems today give every indication of remaining active concerns—unsolved and menacing—with which Americans may have to learn to live for years and even decades.

The basic concerns transcend national boundaries: the explosive expansion of knowledge, the world-wide conflict of ideologies, the alarming rate of growth of the earth's population, the insistent demand for a better life by the great masses of humanity.

The answers to these perplexing problems will, in large part, come from America's universities—the nation's richest resources of learning and research. From them will come the new knowledge and the minds trained to deal with these problems.

But if American universities are to be equal to a challenge of this magnitude, they must be helped to develop their capabilities to the fullest. This is a vast undertaking for the American people.

The most effective way to lift the general level of college education is to raise the standards of the pace-setters—the few prototype institutions which represent the best in American education.

Princeton is one of the comparatively few national institutions which continually raise the sights and point the way for other universities. Thus, the maintenance of its excellence is important not for Princeton alone, but for other institutions of higher learning as well.

---

Reprinted by permission from Princeton University. Referred to on p. 5.

Princeton recognizes, however, that excellence in education is a journey, not a resting place. To stand still is to fall behind. For Princeton to continue to lead today—and tomorrow—it must be materially strengthened.

But crippling financial restrictions stand in the way. Income that was adequate in the past is now a strait jacket. Weakened by inflation, its present resources do not enable Princeton even to hold its own, let alone to move ahead.

Resolved to meet the exacting demands it makes of itself, Princeton refuses to accept these limitations. For the immediate future, therefore, it has launched a program For a Stronger Princeton—an unprecedented appeal for $53 Million for Princeton University.

The success of this forward-looking program will advance Princeton University directly—and the cause of American higher education indirectly—for generations to come.

*Appendix B*

# On The Rise of Schizophrenia
# in the Secretary

*A Study of the "Two-Boss" or "Double-Entendre" Syndrome*

The secretary, especially if abnormally anxious to please or abnormally rebellious—and especially if both—will, under exposure to employers of differing temperaments, develop symptoms expressed by malaise, confusion, and finally, extreme vacillation ending occasionally in total paralysis. As follows:

1. If one boss requires instant and unquestioning obedience punctuated by periods of docile inactivity; and the other boss hopes for initiative and quiet coping. . .

   She gets mixed up.

2. If one boss wants everything filed away and the other wants everything out where he can lay hands on it. . .

   Neither gets either.

3. If one boss wants her to correct sense, punctuation, style, and spelling; and the other desperately wants her not to. . .

   Her copy reflects marked Tremor, Insecurity, and Aphasia.

4. If neither of them wants her in the room with him, and there are two rooms, she develops wheels—sometimes complicated by a tendency to hide in the kitchen. . .

   Unwanted.

5. If, and these cases are fortunately extremely rare, one boss has an intellectual curiosity about the aberrant mentality of his secretary—to which he has contributed—and wants full explanations of

---

Referred to on p. 6.

her behavior; and the other couldn't care less and wants it short and snappy, and the secretary, or as we must now call her, the patient, does not have the quick responses of a hunted fox. . .

She develops a gibber.

Attention to the plight of victims of Secretary's Schizophrenia, Type B&G, is long overdue. Their pitiable condition is commonly exacerbated by an irrational affection for their masters, or monsters, as females who become secretaries are masochistic to start with. . .

God Help Them

*Appendix C*

# A Narrative Beginning for a Brochure

*An Indefinite Future*

On a quiet May evening in 1904, a wealthy American, Ion Perdicaris, was dining with his family on the vine-covered terrace of "The Place of Nightingales," his summer villa on the outskirts of Tangier.

Suddenly, bandits led by the Moroccan chieftain Raisculi swept down from the hills. Perdicaris was kidnapped and held captive as a gesture of defiance to the Sultan of Morocco.

The incident set off a flurry of diplomatic activity. Cable messages flashed back and forth across the oceans. Finally, the diplomatic dialogue ended with an eight-word message from the American Secretary of State to his consul general in Tangier:

"This government wants Perdicaris alive or Raisculi dead."

Perdicaris was freed and the incident soon forgotten—except for the message which was widely attributed to President Theodore Roosevelt. It was considered an example of swift, decisive action in international affairs.

Today, however, this message serves only as a reminder of a past era in which Americans felt supremely confident of their ability to solve whatever problems they were called upon to face.

That era, so warmly tinged with optimism and confidence, is gone. A world war, a depression, a greater war, fission and fusion, new concepts of space and time, a cold war—all these have intervened. To most Americans, nothing seems simple any more. Nothing is black or white, open or shut, either/or.

Americans today are coming to realize that there are no simple solutions to the grave problems that beset our nation as a world power.

These problems are both urgent and perplexing: the ideological struggle that divides the world, the competition for the uncommitted countries, the aspirations of the newly emerging nations, the desires of the great masses of the earth's population for a better life. . .

Incorrigibly optimistic even today, we Americans are sobered and shocked when we recognize that such problems may continue to perplex us indefinitely. We will have to learn to live without the security of final solutions.

---

Reprinted by permission of the Fletcher School of Law and Diplomacy. Referred to on p. 9.

But while the problems cannot be readily solved, they can and must be coped with. How we cope with them in the decade ahead may well prove decisive for our way of life, if not for our very lives.

## A Definite Need

The continuing crisis in world affairs compels this country and all free nations to build anew their economic and military strength. Yet, as Churchill has observed, we arm to negotiate. We must rely as never before on the methods and skills of diplomacy.

For these all-important negotiations, no magic formula exists. Nor is any single diplomatic agreement or triumph likely to assure peace with justice and freedom—the only peace acceptable to us. Such a peace can be built only by patient, skilled diplomacy.

In the unfolding era of uncertainty, the struggle for peace poses unprecedented problems. It will require unprecedented efforts every day, every week, every year, for as far into the future as we can see.

This struggle will demand a new statesmanship in diplomacy geared to the less exact, but more exacting, requirements of an uncertain time. America must raise up a new generation of diplomats equal to the perils—and the opportunities—of their mission.

These new diplomats must possess the inner resources to counter the spiritual exhaustion and mental cynicism that so easily develop when crisis follows crisis, problems defy solution, and accomplishments are severely limited.

Diplomats of this order must be carefully and skillfully developed. The backbone of America's foreign service—the career officers who constitute about 99 per cent of all foreign service officers—is the product of special education and training.

America needs more such men, and better men. We will have them only if we strengthen the schools and training centers where diplomats are developed.

## A Far-Sighted Program

In the forefront of America's training centers for careers in diplomacy and related professions is the Fletcher School of Law and Diplomacy at Tufts University.

Administered by Tufts with the cooperation of Harvard University, the School also benefits from the guidance of a Board of Advisors which presently includes the President of the United States and five past and present American Ambassadors.

From its very inception in 1933, the Fletcher School has pioneered in the training of men and women of outstanding leadership potential whose contribution and impact in world affairs would far exceed their numbers.

It has inspired the founding of other American schools in this vital field, and has provided the leadership for them. The first graduate school of its kind, it has continued to lead the way in educating for careers in diplomacy, international business, journalism and teaching.

The Fletcher School's influence has not been limited to this country; it has truly served the world. Its 1110 living graduates include nationals of 43 other countries. Over the years, it has become the most widely recognized international center for the training of foreign students and mid-career diplomats.

But today the School faces a new challenge and a singular opportunity: to continue its role of leadership by strengthening its services for greater responsibility. In the past, it has worked wonders with the limited resources at its disposal; now, with additional support, it can capitalize on its potentialities for essential service to the nation.

Recognizing the vital mission of the School and the important advantages that additional support will now make possible, Tufts University has made the development of the Fletcher School a major objective of its current campaign for $7,550,000 for the Tufts University Program. The University has allocated $1,377,775 of its total goal for the Fletcher School.

# Flexibility to Meet Your Special Needs

Because your institution is different, your fund-raising problems are different, too. The distinctive feature of Bowen & Gurin's fund-raising service is our flexibility in meeting your unique needs.

The changing nature of philanthropy today requires replacement of standard fund-raising formulae with more imaginative, less doctrinaire development techniques. Our approach enables us to accept a wide range of varied assignments.

We specialize in "shirt-sleeve" counseling—not only advising on policy and procedure but actually assisting in all phases of development, including surveying the needs of an institution, and planning, organizing, and conducting a campaign to meet those needs. Our writing services are considered among the finest in the field; we prepare printed materials, mail appeals, and presentations for foundation, corporate, and government grants.

Your fund-raising program may be managed by a Bowen & Gurin resident director or, with our guidance and assistance, by a member of your own staff. If you do not require continuous service, our part-time or peak-load assistance saves you the expensive and difficult prospect of finding and adding highly skilled personnel to your regular staff.

We offer you the advantage of dealing with the first team—individually and collectively. A partner maintains close and continuous liaison with the firm's account executive and the client. At weekly meetings, all partners and staff members review your program in depth. Additional support is provided, when needed, by our Board of Consultants, selected for their demonstrated competence and leadership in a particular field of fund-raising.

You gain the benefit of our experience in dealing with a wide variety of fund-raising activities in the fields of education, health, and welfare. We also bring to bear on your problems our experience in meeting the public relations needs of foundations, financial institutions, and community and cultural centers.

We work on a retainer or on a project basis, whichever best meets your needs. Monthly retainer fees are based on the number of hours of service required during the month; project charges are carefully estimated on the basis of the number of hours required to complete the assignment. Out-of-pocket expenses incurred on your behalf are billed separately and at cost.

Referred to on pg. 24.

Recognizing the need for new thinking in fund-raising, we are pioneering with a number of clients in a selective approach to continuous capital development, integrating capital campaigns, annual giving, deferred giving, and other fund-raising programs into a long-term development plan. Each of these programs is individually designed; there is no pattern to which a client must conform. While we respect traditional fund-raising principles, we are flexible in applying them and creative in adapting them to your unique needs.

*BOWEN & GURIN, INC.*
801 Second Ave., New York, N.Y. 10017
MUrray Hill 6-1676

Members: American Association of Fund-Raising Counsel
Association of Fund Raising Directors
National Public Relations Council of Health and
Welfare Services
Public Relations Society of America

# For a Brochure to Deliver

"Brochures, like babies, are easy to conceive but hard to deliver" was the thrust of a talk on fund-raising brochures by Robert D. Barnes, partner of the Bowen & Gurin & Barnes firm, as reported by the *FRI Monthly Portfolio*.

"For a brochure to deliver, it must communicate something to somebody. The opposite of the kind of communication we're striving for is found among the Arapesh people of New Guinea. When some event of importance occurs, there are drum beats from hilltop to hilltop.

"But all that the signals convey is that something has happened about which the listeners had better become excited. Too many brochures are of this sort.

"We could profit by the example of the blind beggar. He found his tin cup filled and running over when he changed his sign from 'I am blind' to 'It is springtime and I am blind.'

"Many institutions reject what they consider the 'Madison Avenue approach' by substituting sincerity for ability. It is plainly no more insincere to employ 'techniques' in conveying your message to the public than to employ them in a round of golf."

Reprinted from the *FRI Monthly Portfolio* by permission of the publisher, The Fund Raising Institute. Referred to on p. 32.

*Appendix F*

# British Tax Laws Affecting Charitable Gifts

*(The following is excerpted from a report by John J. Schwartz, president of the American Association of Fund-Raising Counsel, Inc., on his attendance at the Ditchley Foundations Conference on Private Giving in the Light of Changes in Economic and Government Policy, which was held in mid-December 1982 at the Ditchley estate near Oxford, England.)*

In the last two years, substantial changes have been made in the British tax laws affecting charitable contributions. The present convenanting system provides that, if a donor contributes a set amount to a charity for a minimum of four years, the charity receives at the end of the four-year period the tax that the government collected from the donor on the amount of his contribution.

The system thus provides a guaranteed income to a charitable organization; it also, it is claimed, saves fund-raising costs (most Americans present disagreed with this claim on the basis that certainly some donors who potentially could give larger amounts use the covenanting system as an easy way out).

The main criticisms of the covenanting system are that it is much too complicated for the average person, and it does not give sufficient encouragement to giving by lower income donors.

A significant number of taxpayers of high income level now receive an additional tax allowance which, in some cases, can make possible even greater donor benefits than the American tax laws provide. Those below the upper classes tend to consider charity as an activity by the rich for the rich—in the sense that the wealthy benefit more from the tax law.

---

Reprinted by permission of the author. Referred to on p. 52.

*Appendix G*

# Fair Practice Code

1. Members of the Association are firms which are exclusively or primarily organized to provide fund-raising counseling services, feasibility studies, campaign management and related public relations, to nonprofit institutions and agencies seeking philanthropic support. They will not knowingly be used by an organization to induce philanthropically inclined persons to give their money to unworthy causes.

2. While the Association does not prescribe any particular method of calculating fees for its members, the Organization should base its fees on services provided and avoid contracts providing for contingency, commissions or a percentage of funds raised for the client.

The Organization should base its fees on high standards of service, and should not profit, directly or indirectly, from the materials or services billed to the client by a third party. Member firms will not offer or provide the services of professional solicitors.

3. The executive head of a member organization must demonstrate at least a six-year record of continuous experience as a professional in the fund-raising field. This helps to protect the public from those who enter the profession without sufficient competence, experience, or devotion to ideals of public service.

4. The Association looks with disfavor upon firms which use methods harmful to the public, such as making exaggerated claims of past achievements, guaranteeing results, and promising to raise unobtainable sums.

5. No payment in cash or kind shall be made by a member to an officer, director, trustee, or advisor of a philanthropic agency or institution as compensation for using his influence for the engaging of a member for fund-raising counsel.

6. In fairness to all clients, member firms should charge equitable fees for all services with the exception that initial meetings with prospective clients are not usually construed as services.

**American Association of Fund-Raising Counsel, Inc.**

---

Reprinted by permission of the American Association of Fund-Raising Counsel, Inc. Referred to on p. 87.

*Appendix H*

# Some Fund-Raising Changes: A Backward Glance

## by Maurice G. Gurin

At the outset of the 1980s, a number of us fund-raising consultants succumbed to the heady temptation of trying to read the future—to forecast the trends likely to emerge in the decade ahead. With these noble efforts of questionable value behind us, it might be useful now to see if we are clearer in limning the past—to note some of the changes in fund-raising concepts and practices over the past few decades.

Such an endeavor, of course, is also susceptible to error, particularly if it relies (as it does in this case) upon the twin vagaries of memory and impression (what consultant has the time—or indeed the temerity—to test his frail faculties against those of his colleagues?).

The present status of the fund-raising art—its practices still evolving and improving because they have not yet been codified in cement—may permit some of our colleagues to harbor different memories. What follows are some changes that readily come to our mind, and our experience and involvement with them (feigned modesty moves the author to employ the editorial "we" and "our").

### Study Reports

1—The written report of a feasibility study for a capital campaign has shrunk considerably in length. We can remember in the 1950s wrestling with one firm's report that ran over 350 pages. Since then, firms have been less profligate with paper, more thoughtful of volunteers' eyesight and patience.

It is our impression that the written study reports of major fund-raising counseling firms have been greatly shortened without the loss of essential content. What has been eliminated mainly: fat and repetition. What has been gained: clarity and readability.

Our reports ranged from 40 to 60 pages, but even then we wondered whether busy volunteer leaders would read that much. So we started the report with a one-page summary of the study's major conclusions. With

---

Reprinted by permission of the American Association of Fund-Raising Counsel, Inc., publisher of the *AAFRC Review* in which the article originally appeared. Referred to on p. 96.

that safeguard, a volunteer leader who only read the first page had learned the essence of the findings. We also found it a useful discipline; we felt that if we couldn't get the main conclusions on one page, we didn't know what they were. We are certain that other firms employed similar devices.

### Prospect Brochures

2—Fewer institutions embarking on capital campaigns are now producing elaborate and expensive brochures for major gift prospects. These beautifully printed and designed brochures were often perceived as feeding the egos of campaign leadership, were occasionally out of date when they first came off the press, and were frequently viewed as imprudent expenditures for institutions professing to need funds. Many institutions, however, still produce them.

Our preference since the 1960s has been for a case statement prepared to look as if it has been individually typed for the major gift prospect to whom it was personally addressed. Its impact cannot possibly be matched by a printed brochure, which was obviously produced for large numbers of prospects. And now, with word processing machines, it is easy to make changes in a case statement and to produce variations of it to appeal to donors' special interests.

### Volunteer Aids

3—Further refinement has been achieved in developing materials to aid the volunteer solicitor with his prospect assignments. Certainly some firms have made it a practice to re-evaluate and revise the "standard" tools in their solicitor's kit to fit the special circumstances of each new campaign.

The tool to which we have accorded major attention is a one-page outline of the case for the solicitor's use in talking—or preparing to talk—with a prospect. Such a one-pager is particularly useful when the case is complex or its essence needs to be extracted.

4—Even the campaign fact sheet has been compressed—a welcome development—particularly when we have seen as many as five pages masquerading as a fact sheet (a contradiction in terms). How can a one-page fact sheet be reduced in size?

In the 1960s, the University of Pennsylvania (among other institutions) produced a 2½" by 4" fact folder (a 5" by 4" sheet folded in half) that could fit into a flap of a man's wallet. Small as it was, it provided the basic facts not only on the capital campaign, but also on annual giving and bequest income, as well as on the university in general (including the student body, alumni, finances, hospital service, athletics, library system, and employees).

Compact and useful, this fact folder scored big with volunteers, who are so often deluged with more reading material than they either need or can digest. Brief was beautiful; small was smart.

## Campaign Counseling

5—Practically all of the major firms are now providing capital campaign counseling, though a number of them offer it in addition to resident campaign direction.

When the predecessor firm we headed in the 1960s decided to discontinue its resident campaign counseling and provide only campaign counseling, we were alone among the AAFRC firms to take this approach.

Since then, however, campaign counseling has become a recognized and sometimes preferred alternative to resident campaign direction. Contributing importantly to this trend has been the greatly strengthened development staffs at major institutions who are capable of day-to-day campaign management.

6—There is increasing awareness that, in general, an evaluation committee no longer serves a useful function. A possible exception: an organization in "East Succotash" capable of enlisting the services of a leading banker, a widely known accountant, and similar types who know the campaign prospects' financial situations and are willing to rate their giving potential.

We took the position in the past that the evaluation function could best be assumed by the committees that would solicit the prospects. And where solicitors do not know the prospects best, they are not the right solicitors for the prospects.

It also seemed to us that, with effective campaign volunteers usually in short supply, it was inexcusable (except in a small town) to assign any of them to an evaluations committee when they could be more profitably used as solicitors.

7—Strict adherence by fund-raising counseling firms to the "rule of thirds" has certainly diminished. Capital campaign gift tables now are not all constructed (as they were since the mid-1940s) in accordance with this "rule"—a formula based on what was then perceived to be generally applicable campaign experience.

According to the "rule," about 10 donors account for the first third of a campaign goal; about 100 donors provide the second third; and all the remaining donors in the constituency furnish the final third.

More recent experience has shown the need to revise this "rule." For example: an institution's top seven donors could give 60 percent of the goal; and they would have to—if the remaining donors are capable of providing only 40 percent. In this situation (which is not as unusual as it may seem), the "rule of thirds" would serve to reduce their gifts.

Noting that this "rule" had not been formally revised or adapted for current relevance or applicability, we used the medium of a book we wrote in 1980, *What Volunteers Should Know for Successful Fund Raising,* to achieve this purpose. The revised "rule" we proposed was the "specific situation formula," which permits a gift table to be based on the special circumstances of the individual capital campaign.

*Appendix I*

# Thirty Trends in the "New Fund Raising"

## by Maurice G. Gurin

**One:** Government support of educational, health, welfare, civic, and cultural causes is now widely acceptable and accepted. In the past, the "threat" of government support (implying government control) encouraged substantial gifts from conservative donors.

**Two:** There is wide recognition that government must give increasingly greater support to these causes. Among the reasons: the financial needs of these causes have risen sharply, philanthropic support does not seem at all adequate, and the threat of government control has not materialized.

**Three:** In the educational field, it is interesting to note, there is now more government support of private universities and more private support of tax-assisted universities.

**Four:** With the economic strain of the Vietnam war and the major domestic problems, Congress is giving a hard look at tax deductions now permitted by law; some changes in these laws will reduce the effectiveness of this incentive to giving. Fund-raising (and therefore philanthropy) is bound to suffer.

**Five:** There is increasing competition for the philanthropic dollar, though philanthropic giving has been steadily rising (from $10.5 billion in 1963 to $15.8 billion in 1968). There is therefore a greater need (1) to make a stronger case for support by critically evaluating programs and avoiding duplication of the efforts of other agencies; (2) to have effective leadership and dedicated workers; (3) to improve techniques; and (4) to make a cause heard in the general din.

**Six:** Practically every institution and organization recognizes that it needs funds if it is to remain viable and relevant. To need no additional support is to acknowledge a bankruptcy of ideas for service. Increasingly greater income is needed "just to stand still" and not lose ground. This

Reprinted by permission of the Council for Advancement and Support of Education, successor to the now defunct American Alumni Council, the publisher of *Alma Mater*. Referred to on p. 97.

general situation may tend to overwhelm the giving public, confusing them in terms of priorities of need, and making them callous, as they recognize that they cannot support all the appeals.

**Seven:** This same situation has, of course, strengthened the United Fund movement in cities throughout the country, and increased hostility between United Fund adherents and causes campaigning for support independently (such as the American Cancer Society and the American Heart Association).

**Eight:** The computer is starting to be more broadly recognized as an important fund-raising tool. Two ways in which it can help: prospect information can be stored and rapidly retrieved in a number of desirable ways (by age, status, sex, whatever); and computerized mailings provide a more effective and efficient method of fund-raising by mail.

**Nine:** Fund-raisers are acquiring and using management skills. Usually, an institution or organization must have its house in good running order if it is to raise funds effectively. Therefore, the fund-raiser has to know something about management. An obvious example: the members of a Board of Trustees or Directors must be "programmed" for their interest, activity, advocacy, and support even if no capital campaign is contemplated.

**Ten:** The need for greater annual income—whether from endowment or through giving programs—has encouraged exploration of new ways of obtaining funds. One example: a private school with limited funds and means to obtain them, residing in an area which is now mainly a business district, gave a 99-year lease on its valuable property (deeded to the Quaker School by William Penn) to a major corporation which then built a 20-story office building and a school building adjacent to it. Thus, the school building was obtained by the school at no cost, and the office building will eventually provide from its rental income the financial support the school will require for its operations.

**Eleven:** Novel and intriguing innovations are becoming ever more important in attracting substantial gifts. One major donor underwrote the possible loss to an institution which borrowed $1 million to buy a new stock issue; the stock doubled in value in one year and the institution "made" a gift of $1 million in profit.

**Twelve:** Volunteer leaders have far more knowledge of fund-raising than they had in the past; this is all to the good. However, this does not relieve professional fund-raisers of the responsibility of protecting volunteers against misconceptions regarding fund-raising which continue to persist.

**Thirteen:** There is more reliance on professional fund-raisers than ever before. Practically every institution or organization of even modest size has a staff fund-raiser and/or a consultant. This could mean at least two things: competition for the philanthropic dollar should become keener, and volunteer leadership should recognize that fund-raising cannot safely be entrusted to amateurs.

**Fourteen:** The fund-raiser is continuing to lose his anonymity. In years past, he was an almost unseen presence lurking in the backgound, conferring privately with campaign leadership and transmitting his advice indirectly through others. Now, he frequently speaks directly to trustees and campaign leaders, occasionally assists in actual presentations to prospective donors, and when necessary addresses direct appeals to individual prospects and groups.

**Fifteen:** Individuals of top leadership caliber are becoming increasingly overcommitted, and the new generation of philanthropists has not yet made its presence felt. Maybe it is just emerging; and if fund-raisers could assist in bringing them forward, it could be one of our major contributions.

**Sixteen:** Philanthropic work is no longer the special preserve of heiresses and wives of millionnaires. For women, generally, philanthropy is now the established method of achieving social acceptance. It is the fashion— the "in" thing to do—to enlist in a worthwhile cause, to be its advocate, to be shown in one of its activities in the press, and to seek support for its purposes.

**Seventeen:** Student unrest—indeed, all of our social unrest—represents a serious fund-raising problem. We do not yet know to what extent this problem will discourage gifts to universities, but we believe that giving will be adversely affected to some extent in the immediate future.

**Eighteen:** This problem may well affect the role of the university president, who in the past was often selected not only for his academic qualifications but also for his competence in attracting needed financial support. Now, in view of the new university pressures, the university president may need to be a mediator and an interpreter—one who can interpret the young to the old, the university to the state legislature, the teacher to the administrator, the students to the trustees.

**Nineteen:** Capital campaigns seem to be becoming shorter. In the past, a campaign was usually planned in phases: an immediate objectives phase which could be completed in about two years (usually for three-year pledges) and a long-range objectives phase which could be achieved over the balance of the decade. Today, goals which formerly would have been spread over ten tax years are being attempted in two or three years; and, where phases for longer-range objectives are proposed they are limited to five and even three years.

**Twenty:** With continuing inflation and sharply rising building costs, there is now a growing tendency to borrow funds for construction (so building can be started at once) and then to raise the funds to repay the loans. Such borrowed funds frequently come from government, both federal and state. However, it is not unusual for an institution to borrow funds it needs from the outside, rather than tap its endowment funds— and to invest its endowment funds aggressively so as to show a profit after repaying the loan.

**Twenty-one:** Our firm, for one, is dedicated to the principle that a capital campaign should proceed on the basis of a "sequence of events" the achievement of one leading to the start of the next, rather than a concern for calendar or timetable. Prospective donors often have little regard for our schedules; they have their own ideas of when they want to contribute—and their say is final.

**Twenty-two:** Today, there is greater awareness of the vital importance of careful education and cultivation of major prospects before they are solicited. Prospects in this category are too important to be rushed into commitments before they are prepared to pledge at their best, for their gifts comprise the major portion of a capital campaign goal.

**Twenty-three:** We have come to believe that if a major donor responds favorably the first time he is asked, the solicitor has failed to ask for a sufficiently large commitment. The donor should have needed several more visits by the solicitor—and probably consultations with his family, his attorney, and his accountant—if he had been asked for the appropriate gift.

**Twenty-four:** There is a definite trend in capital campaigning now to ask fewer individuals for the larger gifts. Such gifts used to account for about 66 percent of a goal; now they often account for as much as 85 and 90 percent.

**Twenty-five:** There is a companion trend in capital compaigning to involve the balance of an institution's constituency in other forms of support. Thus, the rank and file capable of only modest gifts could be asked to contribute to the capital effort through more substantial gifts to the annual fund—and then to perpetuate their lifetime giving through a bequest.

**Twenty-six:** Annual giving programs, for this and other reasons, have encouraged and received gifts of a size which only recently were considered capital commitments. For example, one university which had previously established a $100-a-Year Club for its alumni has recently established clubs up to the $5,000-a-Year level.

**Twenty-seven:** Capital campaigns, which have run for three or even more years, seem to be setting a pattern for donors' continuing support and thus for increased annual funds for universities and colleges.

**Twenty-eight:** Annual giving programs, it is now more generally recognized, will have to be developed aggressively to provide the annual equivalent of endowment income. Endowment funds are hard to come by; many donors would rather invest their funds and donate the income.

**Twenty-nine:** Aggressive investment management of endowment funds is being explored by forward-looking institutions to provide more substantial annual income for the support of annual operations and possibly for the achievement of capital projects. The Ford Foundation, in particular, has advanced this approach. To date, the market decline has not appreciably discouraged adherents of this approach.

**Thirty:** At least several firms, ours included, believe that a capital campaign once every ten years may have been adequate in the past, but that viable institutions and organizations will soon recognize the need to undertake a program of continuing capital development. A decade is much longer than it once was, and needs are greater and multiply faster. When this need is recognized—and we are doing our part to hasten the day—the traditional differences between capital and annual campaigns will begin to disappear.

*Appendix J*

# Letter to the Editor

To the Editor of the Newsletter:

Anne New's Letter to the Editor in the October 1982 issue merits—and needs—comment. She asks if it is not time to re-examine NSFRE's stand against fund raisers charging on a commission or percentage basis, and she cites two reasons for her inquiry:

1. Sometimes, she notes, the only way a small organization can afford professional fund-raising services is on a commission basis by which the fund raiser would be paid when and if funds are raised and in proportion to the funds raised.

NSFRE's proscription against this practice is contained in its Code of Ethics and Professional Practices, which says that members shall work only for a salary, retainer, or fee. I feel comfortable with a professional society giving *ethical* endorsement to the use of a pre-determined fee, and proscribing against a commission on the basis of *professional* practice. I put this view in this way because I am certain that charging a commission does not advance our *professional* recognition and acceptance.

Ethics is a subject on which people differ. George Bernard Shaw's position, presumably, was that a layman's ethical standards soften as the amount of money involved increases. Surely for fund raisers, the observance of the strictest interpretation of ethical standards is indicated if for no other reason than the close public scrutiny to which fund raising is exposed.

2. Agencies have employed fund raisers on a flat fee basis, Ms. New also notes, "only to find that inadequate funds were raised and that the fee had to be paid, regardless." On the basis of this observation, she states that fees, as well as commissions, are subject to "abuses."

Surely Ms. New knows that an ethical fund raiser cannot guarantee that a desired goal will be achieved; and if there is any question about it, he states this point clearly at the outset of his relationship with an organization. He would certainly be ethical if he recommends a pre-campaign feasibility study and (if a campaign is found to be feasible) he conscientiously puts forth his best efforts to make the campaign succeed.

---

Reprinted by permission from the newsletter of the Greater New York Chapter of the National Society of Fund Raising Executives. Referred to on p. 99.

A campaign goal cannot be achieved solely by the fund raiser; certainly the volunteer leadership has a considerable role to play, and other factors also affect the outcome of a campaign.

A lawyer cannot be faulted for not winning a verdict if he has tried his best; nor can his fee, which he has earned, be withheld. A conscientious fund raiser can be considered to be in a similar position. I do not want to carry this analogy further because a lawyer can—and does—take cases on a commission basis, and sometimes the commissions are astronomical. But the difference here is that lawyers get such commissions from profit-making organizations, and fund raisers serve non-profit organizations.

We all share Ms. New's concern for the small organization that serves a worthwhile cause but cannot afford to pay a fee for fund-raising service— provided, of course, it believes such service is worth paying for and has genuinely tried to obtain the necessary funds. I believe there is a better answer to this problem than providing service on a commission basis. I am sure that I am not the only fund raiser who on occasion has provided free counseling to such an organization.

Whatever "affordability" the commission basis may offer an organization, the practice has not always served an organization's best interests. There have been incidents in which fund raisers working on a commission basis resorted to practices which brought in funds quickly but which adversely affected organizations' relationships in their communities. A fund raiser working on a fee basis has no incentive to resort to such practices.

At a time when organizations' funds generally are inadequate, the public that is called upon for financial support has a right to be particularly interested in their fund-raising expenditures. That public would certainly be more approving of payment for fund-raising service on a fee basis than on commission.

**Maurice G. Gurin**
Past President
Greater New York Chapter

# An Unmailed Letter to *The New York Times*

To the Editor:

The extensive account of the financially-troubled gift-supported arts organizations, which appeared in *The New York Times* on December 4, drew deserved attention to probably the most hard-hit of the private sector agencies. An analysis of the *Times'* report on two of these organizations helps explain why arts groups now find themselves in this unenviable position.

"The Paul Taylor Dance Company," the *Times* noted on page one, "has hired a full-time professional fund raiser for the first time in its 28-year history." This disclosure suggests two questions:

—How long does it take arts groups to recognize that their financial support is important enough to be accorded proper professional attention?

—Do arts groups believe that they must be in deep financial trouble before they consider engaging full-time professional fund raisers?

Almost every financially sound organization today has long availed itself of professional fund-raising direction—just as it has arranged for expert management of a program which required professional planning and supervision.

The answer to the question of whether arts organizations can afford to engage professional fund raisers is this simple: can they afford not to?

Particularly vulnerable today are the smaller and more recently-established arts groups which have depended largely, if not entirely, on government support; their very existence is threatened by the withdrawal of that support. Nonetheless, they are at least partially to blame for their present predicament: they did not prudently use the time during which they were funded by government to broaden the base of their support.

They did not follow the example of the older and better-established organizations, which are now in a stronger financial position because they gave appropriate attention to the solicitation of support from "the private sector"—individual, foundation, and corporate prospects for contributions. After all, philanthropy is still an expression of the private sector despite massive government participation in recent years.

Every organization requiring annual support needs someone on its professional (paid) staff who is—or acts as—a professional fund raiser even if he does no more than coordinate the efforts of the agency's

---

Referred to on pg. 99.

volunteers in seeking contributions. That staff person could even be—and sometimes is—the executive director.

In the sense that the staff person is paid, he is a professional—as opposed to a volunteer who contributes his services. But in another sense, a professional fund raiser is a skilled and experienced practitioner. For fund raising to be successful for an organization, such a practitioner is always advisable and usually essential.

The *Times* article quoted the director of development of the New York City Ballet: "Three years ago, a letter plus a telephone call to a given donor might have done the trick. This year, it has to be a letter plus a personal visit. . ."

This "new" requirement is not new to experienced fund raisers or to successful organizations which have followed their advice. It has long been recognized by professional fund raisers that in-person solicitation is the most effective method of obtaining contributions, particularly substantial contributions. As the development director notes, "There is more work involved. . ." But it is worth the effort—and when more than now?

In recent years, leading fund-raising practitioners and spokesmen for professional fund raisers' societies, such as the American Association of Fund-Raising Counsel, have been urging the smaller and more recently-established groups to organize properly for effective fund raising.

What is apparently happening today is that the depressed economy, rising costs, and shrinking government support are forcing organizations seeking to survive to do what they should have been doing all along:

—determine that their case for support is currently valid (that they are still meeting unmet needs),

—strengthen the fund-raising capability of their boards and include representatives of all appropriate sources of support,

—involve and train their board members and other volunteers in effective fund-raising techniques, and

—avail themselves of the expertise and experience of professional fund raisers in planning and conducting their fund-raising campaigns.

Fund raising for gift-supported organizations today is too serious a business, too crucial to their survival in any acceptable state, to be left completely to the amateur and the neophyte. Even with the services of professional fund raisers, these organizations will still have sufficient challenge to contend with.

**Maurice G. Gurin**
New York, December 6, 1982

# A Strange Encounter on a Train in Which a Warning is Sounded: *Repel a Madison Avenue Invasion*

## As related by Maurice G. Gurin

At the outset, it was reminiscent of the old days I knew on the Orient Express as it started its historic run that, by journey's end, thundered through the Balkans.

I had boarded the Broadway Limited for the first leg of a three-day train trip to service a West Coast client; I had noted with satisfaction the lush appointments of my private sleeping compartment; and I had found my way to the dining car where, ensconced at a table to my liking, I had begun to peruse with pleasure the extensive menu.

But then, without any forewarning, the steward appeared at my side and begged permission to seat a gentleman at my table.

"Of course," I said generously, to hide my resentment at having my privacy invaded. The appearance and bearing of the gentleman (if one could term him such) did little to dispel my displeasure.

His suit jacket had four buttons, an obvious Victorian affectation. His face: a chalk-white blank space with two large black eyes staring out from under heavy brows. His hair varied in color, suggesting a hairpiece that didn't quite match whatever remnants of his own showed through. His moustache, wild and unwieldy, appeared to be less his own than a transparent disguise.

What was most unsettling: he kept eyeing me with a curiosity bordering on impropriety. Finally, in what he must have thought a friendly tone, he said: "May I ask what line of work you pursue?"

"Fund raising," I replied civilly.

"Fund raising?" he asked incredulously.

"Yes, fund raising," I said. "Haven't you ever heard of it?"

"I'm afraid I have," he said. "I'm in it."

He asked for my card and handed me his, which struck me as strange indeed, as it provided no information other than his address. Noting that he domiciled in New Jersey, I managed to suppress the impulse to look superior.

"I place you now," he said. "I thought I knew you. That's why I was staring. I've read you and I've heard you speak. . . A belligerent elder statesman, not quite as dull as some others I've encountered."

"I try," I said, uncertain as to whether I was insulted or complimented.

"The trouble with elder statesmen is that they are so concerned with the long view they don't see the present danger to fund raising." He paused for effect. "It's being invaded."

I had no notion of his meaning but I thought it might be useful to provide an historical context. "In the 1930s through the 1950s, fund raising was invaded by men from the ministry and the YMCAs. Since then, of course, there have been infusions of bright-eyed men and women who have taken college courses in preparation—"

"I don't mean *people*," he interrupted impatiently. "I'm talking about terminology. Terminology from Madison Avenue. Advertising terminology. Insidious, too. It keeps creeping in. And the surprising thing to me is that instead of being resisted by fund raisers, it's being welcomed with open arms."

He had become quite agitated, and in an effort to calm him I said, "I've certainly been aware of the influence of Madison Avenue. In fact, my last two offices were on that very street."

"Bully for you," he said. "Have you heard of marketing?"

"Of course. Marketing, if I recall Webster correctly, is the process of selling and purchasing in a market."

"And what does Webster say about market research?"

"Gathering factual information about consumer preferences for goods and services," I replied smartly.

"Then why in blazes," he asked testily, "are fund raisers falling all over themselves to adopt these terms?"

"You tell me," I said.

"No, you're the guru. You tell me," he demanded.

I could see that there was no way out except to play along with him. "Because they think they are selling goods and services. Because they view a philanthropic cause as a product," I suggested.

"Not bad for starters," he said.

"Because they have been infiltrated by contagious fugitives from advertising who cannot discard their verbal baggage."

"Keep going."

"Because they never heard of 'testing the case' and 'prospect research' or think that 'marketing' and 'market research' are classier terms."

"Classier *commercial* terms," he said. "But you're getting warm."

"Because they think that fund raising, which suffers from public misunderstanding, could improve its image by taking on some of the coloration of Madison Avenue."

"You're improving," he said encouragingly.

"Because they take refuge in terminology. And because new terms give them the illusion of new techniques."

He smiled, and by way of approval he said, "Would a technique by any other name serve as sweetly?"

His agitation had subsided—or so I thought. But it was short-lived. "Fund raisers embrace these advertising terms for all the reasons you cited—and others. Mainly, they have no critical judgment, no ability to evaluate the need for—let alone the applicability of—marketing and market research for fund raising."

He paused momentarily. "And," he resumed, eyeing me sharply, "I'm surprised that a fund raiser of some stature has not made these observations and sounded appropriate warnings. Is there no guardian, no keeper of the flame in fund raising—no agency like the French have for protecting the purity of the language?"

"There is 'A Glossary of Fund-Raising Terms' that was jointly produced in 1975 by the American Association of Fund-Raising Counsel, the National Society of Fund Raisers, and the National Association for Hospital Development. Neither 'marketing' nor 'market research' are listed," I said.

"That can only mean," he noted, "that these terms have infiltrated only in recent years. That means that there is still a chance for logic and purity of our technology—if something is done about it at once."

He kept staring at me almost accusingly. Finally he said what I feared he'd say. "You're the one to do it. You could do an article on the invasion of Madison Avenue terminology that would carry weight and sound the alarm. You have the entree to the important fund-raising publications."

"I appreciate your exaggerated claims for me, but I am not your man." I said.

"Yes, you're the right one for the assignment," he said, completely ignoring my protestation. "You have been innovative. You've stuck your neck out in the past. So you couldn't be accused of being conservative or even reactionary in wanting to preserve the purity of fund raising's verbal armamentarium."

"Now wait one minute—"

"You could use the article to ask one question that could turn the tide," he continued. "One question: 'Specifically, what can marketing and market research do for fund raising that cannot be gained by such established techniques of its own as thorough testing of the case for support, critical scrutiny of an organization's financial needs, systematic identification and evaluation of prospects, measures to increase their interest and support, and the assignment of solicitors considered to be most effective (in person or by phone or mail) in eliciting their contributions?' "

"I do not dispute the validity of the question, but I do not want to precipitate a disagreeable row," I said. "And that, sir, is final."

"Bah," he sneered. "That's the trouble with you old gurus. No guts."

He got up from his chair, gave me a curt nod, and disappeared down the aisle.

I uttered a sigh of profound relief. Train travel, I concluded, isn't as safe as it was in the old days: there's no telling now what manner of individual one is likely to encounter.

*Appendix M*

# What Fund Raisers Should Know About TV Talk Shows

**By Maurice G. Gurin**
President, The Gurin Group, Inc.

If fund raisers or development directors agree to appear on a talk show program on charity and fund raising, they can practically assume it will include some mention of "fund-raising abuses" and "charitable frauds." But if they don't go on the program, then they can lose the opportunity of presenting a balanced view of such charges which, if they have a basis in fact, are so often presented out of all proportion to their significance.

Perhaps a typical experience, which could be instructive, was the "Straight Talk" program on WOR-TV, Channel 9, in New York City, which addressed the subject of charities today and on which E. Burr Gibson, board chairman of Marts & Lundy, Inc., and this writer were asked to appear. The program was aired from 9 AM to 10 AM in mid-November, and tape-recorded three days before it was broadcast.

One day before the program was to be put on tape, Gibson and I were phoned by Marilyn Neckes, Assistant Producer, and asked to be participants; as it happened, our schedules enabled us to accept. When we arrived the following afternoon, we learned that the program was to be in three 20-minute segments, with each segment featuring two different guests.

We both knew the other guests. Just before going on camera, each set of guests met the two hosts of the program, Ms. Phyllis Haynes and Ms. Mary Helen McPhillips, who alternated in putting questions to us.

Guests on the first segment were Ms. Helen O'Rourke of the Council of Better Business Bureaus, and M.C. Van de Workeen of the National Information Bureau. Questions to them focused on the protection of donors.

One question went to the jugular: "Is a lot of fraud being perpetrated or is there the potential for it?"

Both guests explained that their main purpose was only to provide donors with information on organizations seeking their support so that

---

Reprinted by permission of the American Association of Fund-Raising Counsel, Inc., publisher of the *AAFRC Review*, in which the article appeared. Referred to on p. 101.

the donors could make up their own minds. Indeed, Mr. Van de Workeen said that "money has to be spent to raise money and to administer an organization." Both guests set forth their organizations' own guidelines on "reasonable" percentages of funds raised to be allocated to fund raising and to program.

Gibson and I were on the second segment of the program. Questions to us focused mainly—and (we thought) appropriately—on how gift-supported organizations could now raise more funds to help compensate for federal government cutbacks in support. We both advocated observance of basic fund-raising practices, and the avoidance of gimmicks. As an example, I noted that, despite present conditions, The Fresh Air Fund in 1981-82 increased by 11 percent its fund raising over the previous year because it strengthened its case and its board members actively raised funds.

## Commission vs. Flat Fee

But we were also queried about fund-raising abuses and, specifically, about working on a commission basis. We made these points (among others): the few abuses in fund raising get blown up by the media out of all proportion; while some fund raisers may operate on commission, most of us disapproved of that practice and charged on the basis of the time that we and the client agreed should be devoted to a fund-raising effort; that we investigated potential clients (just as they investigated us) to assure ourselves that we approved of their purposes; and that, because we were in business for the long term, we could not afford to operate in any but the most reputable manner.

Guests on the third segment of the program were Daniel Kurtz, Assistant Attorney General, New York State, and Joseph Shea of the State Charities Registration Bureau. They were questioned about the kinds of control they exercised over fund-raising activities in the state and what they could do to correct abuses. Both guests explained in reasoned (and reassuring) terms the character and extent of their functions for the protection of the giving public.

In all, aside from the more lurid phrasing of several questions, the program was a reasonably balanced exploration of the major factors that concern present-day fund raising and the charitable organizations' financial needs.

I later learned from Ms. Neckes that Channel 9's interests in doing this program were three-fold: (1) Are donors giving more in these difficult times to help take up the slack caused by federal government cutbacks in support? (2) How can donors learn whether most of their gifts are used for program? (3) How can potential donors find out about organizations serving causes in which they believe? These questions were addressed in the program.

What, if anything, can we fund raisers learn from this experience?

Obviously, for us, television can be a mixed blessing. We want to use this important communications medium, but we don't want it to use us in ways which don't advance our professional interests and that of our clients. So we must exercise care—but not so cautiously as to preclude us from taking a constructive role.

This means, I believe, that we must participate in TV programs which address "fund-raising abuses" and "charitable frauds"—so that we can be in a position to correct unfounded charges and to present a balanced view of the few charges which have some basis in fact.

And, above all, we must maintain a realistic view of such charges and not become paranoid and assume we are singled out for special persecution—except possibly in isolated "newsworthy" cases. Other professions, let us recognize, come in for their share of attention by the investigative media; certainly this is true of two of the most respected professions: law and medicine.

Participation by fund raisers in TV programs focused on "abuses" and "frauds" is most often the only opportunity they have to bring enlightenment to the public on these subjects—as well as on related subjects of real significance to philanthropy and its fund-raising needs. In contrast, my own efforts to promote TV programs concerned with serious problems of philanthropy today have been less than successful—even on public television; I am sure my efforts have been typical.

Guests were given good recognition during the program. They were introduced at the outset of each segment and their names and affiliations were given again at the close of the segment. Several times during each segment, the names of the guests were flashed on the screen.

*Appendix N*

# Fund Raising by Objective
## by Maurice G. Gurin

Is it always the most effective strategy in raising capital funds to make the case for an institution's total capital objectives—and seek commitments toward their combined achievement? Or is it more effective in some instances to make a case for each individual objective—and embark on *fund raising by objective*?

For decades now there has been an underlying assumption that a stronger case can be made for the whole of an institution's capital objectives than could be made for its individual objectives or even the sum of them.

The sum of the capital objectives for a college, as an example, could include new construction, renovation of existing structures, professorships, and scholarships.

But an overall case statement would not address these objectives as such; rather, it would project an appeal larger than they represent even collectively (the case's motif or thematic catchall could be that education holds the promise of survival in these complex and troubled times). Thus, the achievement of the goal (the combined objectives) could help advance a nationally important cause.

While this conventional approach has included the use of named gift opportunities (to attract major gift prospects with special philanthropic interests), most prospects have been asked to contribute toward the campaign goal—the totality of the objectives as projected by the overall case.

In recent years, this underlying assumption has not been discredited in general; rather, it has been disregarded where it has not proved effective. Particularly in campaigns solely for endowment, institutions have felt the desirability, if not the necessity, of breaking up the entire goal into named gift opportunities and seeking to match them with the interests of prospective donors.

It could be noted that such campaigns are often launched without due regard for their feasibility—for the presence of the essential ingredients of successful fund raising (case, leadership, workers, and prospects of a strength commensurate with the size of the goal). But all organizations do not always follow the fund-raising "book."

It was probably inevitable for the strategy of *fund raising by objective* to start with the endowment campaign, since endowment has proved to have less than irresistible appeal for large numbers of major prospects. Many prospects for such a campaign feel they would be throwing money into an unmarked pot with nothing to show for the substantial gifts they are asked to make (some of them, though they may deny it, want the recognition of named gift opportunities). Other prospects prefer to provide the equivalent of annual income from endowment, and to retain the principal.

Several "theoretical" examples—instances where *fund raising by objective* could be strategically indicated—could be instructive.

A symphony orchestra's campaign solely for endowment could proclaim a general motif (such as the need to maintain its position of leadership among the nation's symphonic orchestras); but the difficulty it could encounter in raising endowment could warrant a campaign strategy of dividing the total campaign goal into disparate and attractive named gift opportunities (such as a distinguished conductors' program) as a more effective way of interesting major donors.

A museum campaign solely for endowment could have greater appeal for major prospects by focusing its case and fund raising on attractive individual capital objectives (such as a new gallery for recent acquisitions).

A public television station's campaign for endowment to fund (or advance funds) for producing programs could find fund raising more effective if it were focused entirely on such named gift opportunities as program series (probably in the areas of public affairs, culture, and education) designed to appeal to the interests of certain individual, corporate and foundation prospects. And, if the program series could be sold to the network or other stations, the costs of the series could be recaptured and revolving funds could be maintained.

A nonprofit repertory theater's campaign for endowment (to function as a working capital fund) could find that attracting capital (or, indeed, any kind of financial support) too often depends upon how much of a "hit" the last production scored. The theater could focus its fund raising for endowment on several series of plays (such as Shakespeare plays, Restoration comedies, and modern classics), each of which could appeal to different categories of prospective donors.

As projected, none of these "theoretical" examples seek endowment for an institution's overall operations and maintenance. However, such endowment could be gained by including in the "pricetags" of the institution's named gift opportunities a proportionate share of its overhead. And while the examples are focused solely on endowment, the *fund raising by objective* approach is equally applicable for such other capital objectives as new construction and renovation (expendable funds).

The individual capital objective would be planned as a separate solicitation effort, with its own specific case, prospects deemed to have a special interest in the objective, and volunteer solicitors likely to be influential with such prospects.

Because prospects would be asked to contribute to objectives of special interest to them, they could be expected to give at their best. By doing so, they would provide a greater share of the total amount of the objective than they would of the much larger amount of a combination of objectives; accordingly, their gratification would be greater and more meaningful.

Not all capital funds in the past have been raised through the medium of a conventional campaign that embraces a number (or "mix") of capital objectives. In some instances, no more was required than the matching of a capital objective with the interest of a single prospect.

The concept of *fund raising by objective*—a selective departure from standard fund-raising practice for an institution which otherwise would incorporate an assortment of objectives into the conventional capital campaign—is advanced here for critical scrutiny and response. This strategic approach is already abroad. Surely others than the author may have advanced it—if not by the name he accords it here.

# Thinking of Becoming a Consultant?

## *(A Checklist for Fund Raisers)*

1. Would you get nervous when Friday comes and there is no paycheck?
2. How long are you prepared to carry yourself financially until you can sign up clients?
3. What counseling services are you qualified to offer gift-supported organizations?
4. Do organizations needing these services represent an adequate prospective client list?
5. Do such organizations ordinarily look to consultants for these services, or do they expect them to be provided by their fund-raising staffs?
6. Are there sufficient consultants to meet the need for these services?
7. How would you fare against the competition of such consultants?
8. Would your past fund-raising experience look impressive to prospective clients?
9. Are you temperamentally suited to be a consultant—i.e., to counsel a number of clients simultaneously?
10. Do you recognize that as a consultant you will be running two businesses: one, serving your clients, and, two, seeking additional clients?
11. Are you prepared to serve out-of-town clients and meet the problems they may represent for you?
12. Are you willing to serve less financially secure organizations at the outset than those for which you may have worked as a staff fund raiser?
13. Have you estimated what you will need in client income to cover your draw, an office, secretarial and professional services, and other business expenses?
14. Have you determined the fees you would charge, and how you would bill for expenses?
15. Are these fees competitive with those of consultants at your level of competence?

---

Referred to on p. 105.

16. Do you intend to be an individual consultant, or to organize a counseling firm(which, of course, entails additional problems of financing, personnel recruitment, and firm management)?
17. Have you planned how you would make known and promote your counseling services?
18. Would it be possible for you to line up one or two clients in advance— while you are still working as a staff fund raiser and without neglecting your present responsibilities?

# Index

# OTHER VALUABLE FUND-RAISING RESOURCES FROM TAFT

## TAFT BASIC II SYSTEM
The ultimate fund-raising resource covering the charitable giving of America's largest foundations and corporations. Consists of a one-year subscription to the Taft Corporate Information System and the Taft Foundation Information System.

## TAFT CORPORATE INFORMATION SYSTEM
Detailed coverage of America's major corporate giving programs—both corporate foundations and direct giving programs. Includes annual 760-page hardbound *Taft Corporate Giving Directory*—biographical data on trustees and officers and current, comprehensive analyses of contributions programs. Exhaustively indexed. Supplemented with monthly newsletters, *Corporate Giving Watch/Corporate Giving Profiles.*

## TAFT FOUNDATION INFORMATION SYSTEM
Detailed coverage of America's major private foundation giving programs. Includes *Taft Foundation Reporter*—annual 800-page hardbound directory with biographical data on foundation trustees and comprehensive reports and analyses of foundation giving programs. Exhaustively indexed. Supplemented with monthly newsletters, *Foundation Giving Watch/Foundation Giving Profiles.*

## PEOPLE IN PHILANTHROPY: A Guide to Nonprofit Leadership and Funding Connections
Formerly titled, *Trustees of Wealth,* this unique directory contains biographical data on the thousands of individuals who control philanthropy in the corporate and foundation world, as well as profiles of many of America's wealthiest individuals.

## HOW TO RATE YOUR DEVELOPMENT OFFICE: A Fund-Raising Primer for the Chief Executive
Outstanding guide covering every detail needed to clarify and assess the success of your development office. Superb manual for every chief executive—whether you're planning to institute a new development program or looking to make your current fund-raising office more productive.

## CORPORATE GIVING YELLOW PAGES: Philanthropic Contact Persons for 1,300 of America's Leading Public and Privately Owned Corporations
Here are hundreds of corporate direct giving programs and corporate foundations *not covered in any other resource!* Lists sponsoring company, contact person, address, and phone number. Indexed by location and type of industry.

## AMERICA'S WEALTHIEST PEOPLE: Their Philanthropic and Nonprofit Affiliations
An invaluable complement to *People in Philanthropy,* this directory focuses in even greater detail on the charitable habits of America's rich. Over 500 in-depth profiles couple biographical data with philanthropic, nonprofit, and corporate affiliations.

## THE 13 MOST COMMON FUND-RAISING MISTAKES and How to Avoid Them
This down-to-earth, witty, cartoon-illustrated book shows how adherence to a few basic principles can yield more grants, more gifts, more wills and bequests. Written by Paul H. Schneiter and Donald T. Nelson, it draws on exceptional experience in legendary Mormon fund-raising circles.

## BUILDING A BETTER BOARD: A Guide to Effective Leadership
For every board member or nonprofit executive interacting with trustees, this succinct booklet will help you gain maximum board effectiveness through understanding the roles and expectations of each and every board member. Written by Andrew Swanson who brings over 25 years of practical working experience as president or trustee on more than 30 nonprofit boards.

## THE PROPOSAL WRITER'S SWIPE FILE: 15 Winning Fund-Raising Proposals
The grants-oriented fund raiser's "best friend" in helping design successful applications. Pattern your proposals on these examples of actual winning proposals.

## PROSPECTING: Searching out the Philanthropic Dollar
The most comprehensive functional manual on donor research available today, covering every major aspect of prospect research. Includes valuable Forms Kit enabling you to conveniently record your prospecting research.

## FUND RAISING FOR PHILANTHROPY
Not just another good book on fund-raising techniques, but straight talk about the fund-raising process in one complete overview. Written by renowned veteran fund raiser Gerald Soroker.

## DO OR DIE: Survival for Nonprofits
For the nonprofit executive who recognizes the advantage of "profit thinking for nonprofit organizations." Insightful exploration of nonprofit management approaches—separates myth from fact.

## UP YOUR ACCOUNTABILITY: How to Up Your Funding Credibility by Upping Your Accounting Ability
The first nontechnical accounting "textbook" ever written specifically to meet the needs of the nonprofit manager or student. Gives you the basic information you need to understand the financial workings of a nonprofit group and to do realistic financial planning.

**DEAR FRIEND: Mastering the Art of Direct Mail Fund Raising**
For the experienced practitioner or those just getting started in raising funds by mail. Written by principals of the renowned Oram Group, Kay Partney Lautman and Henry Goldstein. The outstanding how-to guide.

**THE NONPROFIT EXECUTIVE**
Action-oriented monthly newsletter for nonprofit managers. The first newsletter dedicated to advancing the careers of executive-level nonprofit managers and development officers. Your way of keeping in touch with all the trends, new development ideas, events, and concepts that affect your performance and success. Features a special careers/jobs section.

For more information call TOLL FREE 800-424-3761.